THE CONCRETE ENEMA

And Other News of the Weird Classics

THE CONCRETE ENEMA

And Other News of the Weird Classics

BY CHUCK SHEPHERD

ANDREWS AND McMEEL
A Universal Press Syndicate Company
Kansas City

ISBN 0–8362–2181–8

Library of Congress Catalog Card Number: 96-84107

Attention: Schools and Businesses

Andrews and McMeel books are available at quantity discounts
with bulk purchase for educational, business,
or sales promotional use.
For information, please write to: Special Sales Department,
Andrews and McMeel, 4520 Main Street, Kansas City, Missouri 64111.

Contents

Foreword

We must treasure the things that bring us close to the roots of life: sleeping under the stars and waking to the symphony of nature. Watching a child build sand castles. Reading News of the Weird.

For it is here, in Chuck Shepherd's "abstract and brief chronicle of our time," as Shakespeare eloquently put it in his review of News of the Weird, that we see man in his purest, most natural state: walking into trees, setting his head on fire, declaring that Chucky (the dummy, not Mr. Shepherd) talked him into murdering the local priest.

The great social and scientific achievements of mankind have been accomplished in spite of, not because of, our instincts.

Left on its own, nature leads us to beat up our neighbors, fart, worship anything shiny, and most of all assume that others are even more gullible than ourselves.

Though it's nice to imagine that crooks are all athletic French women in black leotards who disable infrared burglar alarms with purse mirrors and rappel into mansions from skylights, filching ill-gotten rubies from fat cats who deserve to lose them, that's not a very realistic picture. Real crooks are bozos, too stupid to be able to make a living without hurting other people. Shepherd tells us about the robbers who hold up armored cars before the pickup (and get away with empty moneybags); murderers who chop off people's heads, then plead insanity because only a crazy person would chop off somebody's head; defendants who think judges will be more kindly disposed to someone who confesses in rhyme, or who claim to be allergic to court-houses, or who try to win the jury's esteem by dressing in Ku Klux Klan robes and being addressed as "Hi Hitler."

Now I'm also quite a fan of both good slapstick and hor-ror, and Shepherd's got those covered as well. Consider, for example, the Canadian man who, in spite of his hosts' re-peated warnings, kept jumping off their roof into the swim-ming pool until he broke his neck. That's the slapstick part. The horror part is that the neck-breaker then sued his hosts for two million dollars—and won.

If you are a politically correct twit, I suggest you drop this book like a hot potato. For in News of the Weird you will find stories about how human beings have been killed by endangered species, and endangered species have been knocked off by environmentalists. If you're a bluestocking, you may not want to know about what the camel did with the fire hydrant. If you like to think that justice in this world is swift and certain, look elsewhere. For in News of the Weird, you will learn about laws that require the stages of striptease joints to have wheelchair ramps (so that all the disabled nude dancers can make it to the stage); that allowed gamblers in New Mexico to sue ATM networks for providing them with cash that they then lost at the craps table; that let a football player sue another football player because he got hurt while being tackled.

But if you love humanity for its entertainment value and want to become a more informed citizen of this nutty planet, curl up with these stories. They will make you feel proud that, no matter how bad your day was, at least you didn't electrocute yourself while trying to cook an eel by plugging it into a wall socket.

Teller
(of Penn & Teller)
April 1996

Introduction

Welcome to the fifth in the series of news compilations that proves that it's not really you, it's the other people. They've taken over; stuff happens to them. You thought your life was a little messed up, but actually, you're in the catbird seat. Furthermore, I say to you from my vantage point: It looks like things are getting worse. (Fortunately.)

Readers of the News of the Weird series (*News of the Weird* by Chuck Shepherd, John J. Kohut, and Roland Sweet, Plume Books, 1989; *More News of the Weird* by Shepherd, Kohut, and Sweet, Plume Books, 1990; *Beyond News of the Weird* by Shepherd, Kohut, and Sweet, Plume Books, 1991; and *America's Least Competent Criminals* by Chuck Shepherd, HarperPerennial, 1993) will not see any of those nearly two thousand stories repeated here, because I don't need to repeat stories. Different things happen, just as ridiculous, just as disturbing:

- Exciting new ways for people to screw up
- Dynamic new sexual perversions

- Creative new plans and schemes that backfire
- Innovative products and services for questionable
  target audiences
- New frontiers in neurotic and sociopathic behavior
- Thrilling new jobs that make you actually love the one
  you have
- Delightful new efforts by people to evade responsibility
- Exhilarating new ways of spiritual expression
- Inspiring new ways to, well, expire
- and much more.

Newcomers to News of the Weird, though, must under-
stand a few things first.

For my money, there are two—and only two—kinds of
people in the world: those who prefer made-up jokes (em-
bellished to the full extent of the storyteller's creativity) and
those who prefer to hear the disturbing, absurd, ironic
things that really happen to real people. The human imagination versus the human experience. If you're in the former
group, you might not "get" a lot of this stuff. You probably
don't have the frequent epiphanies over these stories that
the rest of us have. On behalf of those of us who wallow in
true stories, let me say that we feel sorry for you. There is
little in life more delicious than picturing the participants

in these news stories at the very moment that it dawns on them that they've got a problem. Whether our reaction is the Raucous Laugh, the Sly Smile, the Rolled Eyes, the Slowly Shaken Head, the Lifted Brow, or the Stunned Wince, the moment is electric. Fiction is fine, but it has always been easier to tell an elaborate lie than the elaborate truth. (And, if you're dissatisfied with what you've imagined, you're not stuck with it like you are with reality.) But the authenticity of one's view of the world is necessarily heightened if the component experiences are authentic, too; you can trust reality a lot more than you can trust your imagination.

Of course, for those of you who prefer made-up things, you can probably pick up a copy of the twenty-sixth volume of *Still More Dirty Jokes,* or some such book, wherever you purchased this book. If you want to join the hundreds of thousands of readers* who find News of the Weird therapeutic, you can read it weekly (twelve to fifteen of the best recent stories) in newspapers in over two hundred cities in the United States and Canada or on CompuServe.

*Why not millions? Well, it might be millions, but the way the world is working lately, I have a hard time believing that you and I are members of a very large group.

The
Concrete
Enema

For the even more serious, there are Weird Newsletters: *News of the Weird* (reprints of the weekly column), the *View from the Ledge* 'zine, now in its seventeenth year (things I probably couldn't get past newspaper editors to put in the column), and *Planet Chuck Weekly* (a news review of the steady and joyful decline of America and the world). Get the details, or get News of the Weird's Web site location, or pass along your favorite weird news, or just shoot the breeze, either at P.O. Box 8306, St. Petersburg, FL 33738 or CShepherd@igc.apc.org.

Enjoy, and remember, above all else: It's not us; it's them.

Chuck Shepherd
St. Petersburg, Florida
April 1996

Acknowledgments

I have been compiling weird news formally since 1980 and along the way have acquired many correspondents, the vast majority of whom I have never met. I love them all. They and I have in common a belief that, regardless of Bosnia, budget balancing, etc., the weird news must be reported. Perhaps as a consequence of their gift of single-minded, laserlike ability to spot the really important news, some may themselves be in need of counseling. If you run into any News of the Weird correspondents, I urge that you express your admiration for them, and your sympathy. I can't think of everyone, but here are many of them.

The News of the Weird Board of Editorial Advisers: Chief Correspondents: Myra Linden (New Mexico), Barbara McDonald (Missouri), and Chip Rogers (Ohio).

Senior Advisers: Kenneth Anger (California), Jenny Beatty (Nevada), Gaal Shepherd Crowl (Vermont), Geoffrey Egan (Canada), Leslie Goodman-Malamuth (Washington, D.C.), Ivan Katz (Connecticut), Bob Jones (Washington,

The
Concrete
Enema

D.C.), Richard Kline (Pennsylvania), John J. Kohut (Washington, D.C.), Steve Lauria (New Jersey), Matt Mirapaul (Illinois), and Roland Sweet (Virginia).

The Bureaus: Far East (Bob Brown), Canada (Wolf Kirchmeir, Wendy Middleton, Colleen Peck), Massachusetts (Michael Colpitts), Rhode Island (Paul Di Filippo), Vermont (Bob McCabe), New York (Herb Jue), New Jersey (Walter Maier), Maryland (Robin Andersen), Washington, D.C. (Jim Sweeney, Yvonne Pover, Catherine Stanton, Scott Langill), Virginia (Marty Turnauer), North Carolina (Father Sam Gaines, Harry Lewis), Florida (Linda Phillips, Lurene Haines, J. Michael Lenninger, Mark Garrett), Alabama (Emory Kimbrough, Boyd Campbell), Arkansas (Ruth Czirr, Bill Woodyard, Terry Johnson), Tennessee (Maurine Taylor, Debby Stirling, Steve Johnson, Paul Miller), Kentucky (Debbie Weeter, Jennifer Burchett), Ohio (Susan Zurcher), Illinois (Jerry Pohlen, Michael Smith, J.B. Smetana, Tim Dorr, John Peterson, John Pell, Pat Washburn, Jerry Whittle), Minnesota (Susan Kennedy, Dick Kantrud), North Dakota (Les Loble), South Dakota (Fritz Gritzner), Iowa (Cindy Hildebrand), Kansas City (Paul Schaefer, Brian Wilson), Oklahoma (Robert Lacy, Peter Smagorinsky), Texas (Jim Ferguson, Mark Weiss, H.

Thompson, Allen Pasternak, Charles Tooke), Colorado (Joe
Schwind), Arizona (Lee Sechrest, Tony Tellier), California
(Barbara Tyger, Diane Marcus Fine, Linda Cunningham,
Elyse Versé, Donald Bloss, Aurlie McCrea, Willard Wheeler,
Thomas Slone, Bill Wauters), Oregon (Rhobie Parker,
Michael Bergman), Washington (Elliott Woodward, Pete
Lineberger).

Even though I know I have missed about a dozen people
whom I should have kept better track of, this is the list of
those who contributed stories in this volume, and many of
them have been outstanding Weird Newshounds over the
years:

Gary Abbott, Martha Hearon Adcock, Lindapearl Anderson, Bill Apt, Tom Arnold, George Barnett, Jim Beamesderfer, Janet Beatty, Patrick Bishop, Chuck Blanco, Frank Bosha, D. Brazen, Joan Brennan, Dennis Brothers, John Burrell, John Trapper Byrne, Alice Carnes, Debbie Caviness, Steve Chmela, George Christensen, Keith Clark, Corey Corbin, L. Couture, Virginia Crawford, Eddie Cress, Kurt Darr, David Dellenback, Drew DeSilver, Dena Dickinson, Eric Doner, George Duncan, David Durfee, Heidi Eckroth, Cheryl Eger, Jamie Elvebak, Mike Farrell, Fred Fox, Dan Free, Annette Friedman, Michael Fumento, Andrea Gaines,

The Concrete Enema

Elizabeth Gallas, Michael Garrett, Margie Grasberger, Marilyn Green, Darrell Guessford, Eric Haines, Baxter Harris, Tom Hawkinson, Mrs. Gertrude Hebert, Dr. Steven Hill, Ted Hornbein, Paul Jones, Edward Kimball, Laurie Larson, Donald Lewis, Michael Lewyn, Nancy Liljequist, Tim Maloney, Mark Mason, Peter McCarthy, John McClay, Anne McDermott, Bruce McMahon, George Meitzner, Doug Middleton, Brian Minsker, Donald Mitchell, Steve Morgan, Mike Morton, Richard Morton, Leila Mustachi, Tom Nawalinski, Ray Nelke, Chris Palermo, Matt Paust, Henry Pellerin, David Raney, Richard Raschke, Mary Motlow Richman, Saul Rosenberg, Julius Rosenwald, Jay Russell, Scott Sandbrink, David Schermbrucker, Jack Shafer, Lloyd Shand, E. Shaver, C.C. Shepherd, Greg Siegrist, Margaret Simmons, Gerald Smilay, Martin Avery Snyder, Alan Staley, Allan Stanleigh, Holly Stinson, Gerald Swick, E. Tarlton, Rick Thaler, Nancy Thompson, Christine Van Lenten, Elizabeth Vantine, Sparky Whitcomb, Paul Wishak, Matt Zimmer.

The following people have made many excellent contributions to News of the Weird over the years:

Lage Andersen, Paul Bogrow, Dan Brennan, Stephanie Clipper, Sharon Corbett, Craig Cramer, Michael d'Amico, Henrietta Davis, Jay Ducharme, Harry Farkas, Marie

Gerules, Barbara Gudenius, Seth Hawkins, Mr. and Mrs. "Ted" Henderson, Dorothy John, Chuck Jones, Jim Kane, C. J. Kilgore, Bruce Lemke, Donald Lewis, Marc McDonald, David Menconi, Ronda Messick, Bevo Morris, Jeanette Morrison, Ken Nahigian, Phil Parker, Mrs. Mary Parry, Edward O. Phillips, Billie Schwarz, Wes Simpson, Warren Smith, Milford Sprecher, Steve Swanson, Miss Annie Thames, Will and Chris Ward, Tracy Westen, David Wolf, William C. Young.

And I acknowledge Editors Emeritus—saviors from the early years of News of the Weird—Paul Evans, Steve Magnuson, Kevin Walsh, and Elaine Weiss; the founder of this whole project, Bob Maslow; and two superior Weird News Rangers who passed away in 1995, Glenn McWane and Claude Rinehardt.

I would like to give special thanks to Kelly DeYoe, who operates the News of the Weird Internet site and e-mail list; to the premier salesman in this galaxy, Dan Dalton; and to Dave Nuttycombe, a man of vast talents who periodically lowers himself to paste up the *News of the Weird* newsletter.

THE CONCRETE ENEMA

And Other News
of the Weird Classics

Can't Possibly Be True

☞ In 1991, residents of Port Arthur, Texas, finally convinced Fina Inc., operator of a smelly refinery, to buy
out their land after years of campaigning. Among the
reasons for the residents' success, according to *The Wall
Street Journal,* was a media campaign highlighting the
poor air quality in the neighborhood, dramatized at
media events by one homeowner who possessed the
unique ability to vomit on cue.

☞ Milford, Utah, high school teacher Cherry Florence was
fired in 1992 for misusing results of the school's health
questionnaires about student sexual activity. Florence
released to her classes the names of the school's 170
professed virgins.

☞ Tass news agency reported in 1992 that Olga Franke-
vich, who fled from Soviet security police in 1947 during
the Stalinist purge, surfaced from a house in western
Ukraine, where she had been hiding, mostly under a

bed, for forty-five years. Her slightly bolder sister roamed the house but never left it.

☞ Reuters reported in 1992 that Russian faith healer Boris Zolotov had become popular for his traveling seminars in which he induced mass orgasms in women by mental telepathy. Typically, he began a session by shouting, "Who wants an orgasm?" and dozens of women would yell back, "I do." With throbbing-beat music in the background, he encouraged women to throw themselves into a heap in the center of the room while he chanted and implored them to move feverishly. At a session in Zelenograd, the Reuters reporter wrote that "[a]bout thirty appear to have had a sexual climax."

☞ In Chicago in 1992, Frank D. Zeffere III filed a lawsuit for $40,000 in lost courting expenses against a woman who had broken off their engagement. However, Zeffere, who is a lawyer, wrote her a charming letter, offering to reconcile: "I am still willing to marry you on the conditions hereinbelow set forth. . . . Please feel free to call me if you have any questions or would like to discuss any of the matters addressed herein. Sincerely, Frank."

☞ Actress Mariel Hemingway told *McCall's* magazine in a 1993 interview that she maintains a healthy lifestyle—no drugs, alcohol, dairy, meat, bread, sugar, or eggs, but lots of vegetables, grains, and homeopathic remedies. Furthermore, she said, she replaced her large-sized breast implants with smaller ones.

Can't Possibly Be True

☞ Former Hemet, California, high school quarterback A.T. Page, who had sex over a hundred times with the wife of his coach, Randy Brown, in Brown's presence, said in 1993 that Brown called the adventures "astronaut training" and said the sex would make Page a better football player. Said Page, "Just as [sex] would be going on with [Mrs. Brown], [the coach] would plug in a videotape of a scrimmage or a practice and say, 'Now this is what you're doing wrong [on the field], A.T.'"

☞ The *Los Angeles Times* mentioned in 1993 that the Novel Café in Santa Monica featured Kopi Luwak, the Sumatran coffee reputed to be the world's most expensive, at $130 per pound. According to the café's owners, a certain kangaroolike Sumatran animal eats only the "ripest, best" coffee cherries, digests them, and excretes them, after which natives pick the beans and wash and process them into Kopi Luwak.

☞ At the Bowery subway station in New York City in 1992, Darryl Washington and Maria Ramos were injured when a train plowed into them as they were having sex while lying on a mattress on the tracks. Washington suffered several fractured bones, but Ramos got off with only minor cuts because the quick-acting motorman was able to slow the train. Nonetheless, the couple filed a lawsuit against the Transit Authority for "carelessness, reckless-ness, and negligence" in failing to see them in time. Said the couple's attorney, "Homeless people are allowed to have sex, too."

☞ In 1992, the Pro-Line Cap Company of Fort Worth, Texas, was cited by the Occupational Safety and Health Administration for having inadequate rest room facilities for its female employees. Shortly afterward, according to an Equal Employment Opportunity Commission com-plaint, the company, rather than add the rest room facili-ties, merely fired its thirty female employees.

☞ The New York *Daily News* reported in 1994 on a cell-block fight between murderers Colin Ferguson and Joel Rifkin at the Nassau County Jail. Reportedly, Ferguson, on the telephone, told Rifkin to be quiet. According to the *Daily News* source, Ferguson then said, "I wiped out six devils [white people], and you only killed women." Rifkin allegedly responded, "Yeah, but I had more victims." Ferguson then allegedly punched Rifkin in the mouth.

☞ *The Boston Globe* reported in 1994 that Eulalia Rodriguez and her extended family receive government assistance payments totaling nearly $1 million a year. Rodriguez, who has been on public assistance for twenty-six years, has fourteen children on welfare, seventy-four grandchildren, and fifteen great-grandchildren. Said she, "I'm sick of people acting like I'm some crook. We've got a lot of kids to feed." Rodriguez lives in a six-bedroom, three-story apartment in a gated Boston community called Harbor Point.

☞ A 1992 issue of the *Gaston* (N.C.) *Gazette*, featuring local "People Who Made It" (artists, teachers, business

leaders, athletes, etc.), included Virgil Griffin for his
prominence in the state Ku Klux Klan.

☞ In 1993 convicted California serial killer Randy Kraft
filed a $60 million lawsuit against Warner Books and
author Dennis McDougal, arguing that their book *Angel
of Darkness* defamed him. Kraft, who is on death row for
the sexual torture-murder of sixteen men, said the book
unfairly portrays him as a "sick, twisted" man.

☞ Nude dancer Dora Oberling, thirty, recovered nicely
from a gunshot wound inflicted by a seventy-five-year-
old man during an argument outside the Mons Venus
Club in Tampa, Florida, in 1993. Tampa police sergeant
M.D. Smith said that paramedics treating Oberling told
him that her breast implants "might have saved her life"
by slightly deflecting the bullet aimed at her chest.

Cries for Help

☞ Joseph Randall Davis, thirty-three, was charged with burglary and DUI in Knoxville, Tennessee, in 1993. At his arrest and long afterward, Davis insisted that he is actually a feral cat that should be relegated to the woods instead of jail—and that if the government has any reason to supervise him it should only be to require him to wear gloves because of his dangerous claws.

☞ Rhode Island state police detective Brendan Doherty arrested Albert LaBonte in Providence in 1992 and charged him with impersonating a certain state police officer, namely Doherty himself, for the previous five years. Apparently, LaBonte had seen Doherty on *Late Night with David Letterman* in 1987 and become infatuated; LaBonte had a photograph on his wall from that show of Doherty and other police officers modeling uniforms.

☞ A West Chester, Pennsylvania, urologist reported in a 1991 issue of *Medical Aspects of Human Sexuality* that a man had checked himself into an emergency room suffering from a swollen and lacerated scrotum. Days after the doctor repaired the scrotum, the man confided that he had been masturbating by holding his penis against the canvas drive-belt of a piece of machinery at work during his lunch hour when he leaned too close as he approached orgasm and suffered an industrial accident. Furthermore, he then used a heavy-duty staple gun to close his wound.

☞ In Bloomfield, New Mexico, in 1992, Laura Thorpe, thirty-nine, who said she was frustrated in dealing with physicians about her breast implants, removed them by herself. Using a disposable razor, she cut one breast, then squeezed the silicone gel out. She then passed out but came to several hours later and completed the same procedure on the other breast. The next day, a physician removed the bags and, according to Thorpe, complimented her on her handiwork.

☞ In 1993, Elk River, Minnesota, landlord Todd Plaisted reported that his tenant Kenneth Lane had fled the area, abandoning his rented farmhouse and leaving behind at least four hundred tons of used carpeting, at least ten thousand plastic windows from Northwest Airlines planes, and rooms full of sofas, mattresses, and washing machines, among other things. Lane had told townspeople he ran a "recycling" company, and though there was plenty of intake, there was no evidence of sales. A deputy sheriff driving by the farmhouse earlier had seen Lane burying carpeting with a tractor and had struck up a conversation. The deputy quoted Lane as saying, "I don't know what to say. You got me. I can't even make up an excuse." However, since Lane did not appear to be breaking any law, the deputy did not follow up.

☞ Georgia state representative Jimmy Benefield, fifty-two, admitted in 1993 that he had brought a dildo onto the floor of the legislature. (However, he denied he showed it to the fourteen-year-old legislative assistant who initially reported it.) According to two lobbyists, Benefield occasionally walked around the halls wearing the dildo, covered by an apron over his suit, and flashing it at passersby.

☞ From November 1993 through February 1994, Brenda Butler Bryant filed 335 lawsuits in federal court in Philadelphia, accounting for one-fifth of all new cases during that time; each one, said Judge Jay Waldman, was "frivolous" and unintelligible. He quoted from one Bryant lawsuit against the Social Security Administration: "Big Mac? Slave Master Now? No slave ain't master now. Ride them cowboy. Terrorist, radicals, and militants in authoritative roles to provoke violent crimes Cecil B. Moore." Several filings included, as co-plaintiffs, the Pep Boys, whom Bryant described as her sons.

☞ In 1994, a jury in Canton, Ohio, convicted Estella Sexton, forty-seven, of sexually abusing a thirteen-year-old daughter, one of her eleven children. According to another child, father Eddie Sexton, who is serving a murder sentence in Florida, conducted satanic séances featuring cat carcasses and the spirits of dead relatives. Another child, Pixie Sexton-Good, had recently pleaded guilty in Florida in the death of her infant son and agreed to testify against father Eddie and one of her brothers in a later trial against Eddie for the death of

Pixie's husband, Joel Good. Furthermore, according to other siblings, the dead infant itself was fathered by Eddie, but Eddie said another of Pixie's brothers did it.

Police Blotter

☞ As a spectator at a high school basketball game in 1992, Oklahoma City police officer Eldridge Wyatt became dissatisfied that no fouls were being called on "number 21" and walked onto the court to point out the player's elbowing to the referees. When referee Stan Guffey told Wyatt to leave the officiating to him, Wyatt arrested Guffey. After a few minutes, Wyatt uncuffed Guffey so that the game could continue, but when a reporter asked Wyatt after the game what had happened, Wyatt tried to arrest him, too.

☞ Among the best 911 calls reported over the last few years were the one in 1992 in Salt Lake City by a twenty-seven-year-old woman who was complaining that her husband refused to have sex with her until the Utah Jazz basketball game was over, and one by a twenty-eight-year-old woman in Houma, Louisiana, who wanted police help because her husband was preventing her from watching the season finale of *Knots Landing*.

☞ Michael A. Dittmer, twenty-eight, was arrested in Madison, Wisconsin, in 1992 after police observed him weaving erratically over the road and chased him home. As Dittmer drove into his garage and lowered the door, officer Bart O'Shea drove his cruiser in behind Dittmer's car to prevent the door from closing. According to the officer, Dittmer argued that he could not be arrested because he had made it home before O'Shea could catch him.

☞ David Bridges, twenty-four, was arrested in Grapevine, Texas, in 1993 and charged with stealing a television set from a home. That getaway had been successful, but he was caught and arrested after he went back to the home because he had forgotten the remote control.

☞ Eyeballs in the news: Police in El Cerrito, California, sought Aaron Levall Harris on suspicion of assault in early 1993. At the crime scene was an artificial eyeball with Harris's name on it, which police say might have fallen out during the escape. And in 1993 in Jerusalem, a fifty-year-old man, running from police but finally cornered, took out his artificial eye and threw it at them.

☞ Victor Shaw, fifty-six, was arrested near White River Junction, Vermont, in 1994 after trying to break through a police "rolling roadblock" on Interstate 89. Shaw, who was charged with DUI and other offenses, said, "I saw it so many times in the movies [drivers trying to break through roadblocks] I had to try it."

☞ In 1991, Winchester, Virginia, sheriff's deputies, all males, went public with their complaints that Sheriff Chuck Sturdivant (running for reelection to a second four-year term) was constantly kissing them in public as an expression of professional fondness. Sturdivant, a Republican, was married, the father of two, and hetero-sexual, he said, but explained that he has kissed men for all the years he has been a sheriff and, before that, a deputy. He lost the election.

☞ In 1993 in Bristol, Connecticut, Kathleen Driscoll filed a formal complaint accusing ex-lover Richard LaMothe of being the person who made a series of harassing phone calls to her. In addition to telephone company records that tended to support her charge, Driscoll said that one call consisted only of silence punctuated by a very large belch, which Driscoll positively identified as LaMothe's.

☞ In 1994, the Kansas Bureau of Investigation used laser light technology to identify the prime suspect in a hit-and-run injury in rural Johnson County. Although witnesses said only that the hit-and-run vehicle was a black hatchback, bureau investigators found that the collision was so hard that the first two numbers of the license plate and the month of expiration were imprinted on the victim's pants, and the only black hatchback with those numbers belonged to a fifty-one-year-old man, who was arrested.

☞ The *Salt Lake Tribune* reported in 1993 that officer N.S. Hall had recently arrested two men for engaging in sex in a car in Ogden, Utah, and had taken them to the police station. Due to a processing error at the station, the men were locked up in the same cell and immediately began having sex again.

☞ In New York City in 1992, car passenger José Rodriguez, sixty-nine, got behind the wheel and mowed down nine pedestrians in midtown Manhattan at the height of rush hour. According to his nephew, Rodriguez took the wheel only reluctantly. The car was parked at a curb with Rodriguez waiting for the driver to return, and a traffic officer ordered Rodriguez to move it. Rodriguez protested, but finally obliged the officer—even though he did not know how to drive.

☞ Santa Cruz, California, jail inmate Darrell Lyons was rearrested in 1991 and charged with attempted escape, when a routine X ray turned up evidence of a paper clip in his rectum. Sheriff's deputy Ray Flores said he made the quick arrest "because I could not think of any logical reason for having a paper clip up one's rectum except for the purpose of using said paper clip for the purpose of attempt to escape."

Courthouse Follies

☞ In 1991, Memphis judge Joe B. Brown gave burglar Carlos Haley, twenty, a choice: go to prison or make restitution to his victim. Haley took the latter, and Brown authorized Haley's victim, Prentiss Robbins, to visit Haley's home and take any five items of his choice.

☞ To resolve a 1991 neighborhood noise dispute in San Luis Obispo, California, municipal judge Donald Umhofer ruled that the three basset hounds belonging to Bruce and Brigitte Howey would be allowed to bark only once an hour, for no more than two minutes at a time, and must remain silent from 8 P.M. until 8 A.M.

☞ In 1992, the Arkansas Supreme Court affirmed the rape conviction in *Morgan* v. *State*. Morgan had argued for a mistrial because of a bad decision he made at trial: Over the judge's protest, he had shown his unerect penis to the jury—and then argued that it was proof that he was therefore incapable of the erection necessary to commit rape.

The Concrete Enema

☞ In 1993, Atlanta, Georgia, attorney Dennis Scheib stopped by the prosecutor's office in the courthouse, on his way to represent a new client in a criminal case. Just outside the office, he saw two officers chasing a man down the hall, and he joined in to help. After the three men caught the escapee and handcuffed him, Scheib learned the man was the client he had been on his way to court to represent.

☞ David Rodgers, twenty-two, was charged with animal cruelty after police said he had flushed his pet python down the toilet. The python survived, and Rodgers staged a reenactment of the incident in an Ottawa, Ontario, courtroom in 1992, bringing in a tub and a toilet to prove his innocence. Rodgers said he normally tries to keep the snake in warm water in the bathtub but that it prefers the toilet and had slithered in voluntarily. In the courtroom reenactment, the snake quickly slithered from the tub to the toilet, and Rodgers was acquitted.

☞ A Cincinnati woman charged that a forty-two-year-old man sexually assaulted her after taking advantage of a medical condition that usually causes her to faint when

she hears the word "sex." Allegedly, the man accosted
her in her apartment building, uttered the magic word,
and then assaulted her after she fell to the floor. In a
court appearance in 1993, the woman fainted twice
when prosecutors used the word "sex" in descriptions
of her condition.

☞ Upon hearing his sentence (of sixty days in jail for violating previous DUI sentences) in a Redmond, Washington, courtroom in 1993, defendant Larry Michael Key
broke free and dashed out the door, but Judge Will
O'Roarty leaped from the judge's bench in hot pursuit,
his judicial robe flapping behind him. The judge fol-
lowed Key out of the building, down the street, and into
a supermarket, where a clerk and police captured him.
(After bringing Key back to the courtroom, Judge
O'Roarty tacked on nine more months.)

☞ In 1993: A defense lawyer in San Francisco attempted to
call a parrot to the witness stand on the chance that it
might speak the name of the man who killed its owner,
but the judge said no. And a police dog took the stand in
a Pittsburgh, Pennsylvania, courtroom as a defense attor-

ney tried to show that the dog, and not his client, was the aggressor in a fight. (In another case that year, a chicken took the stand in a Tyler, Texas, courtroom, as part of a suit concerning the effects of chicken vaccinations on the plaintiff.)

☞ In 1992, the families of Michael and Susan MacIvor went to court in Tavernier, Florida, over which family would get Michael's estate. The crucial legal question was which of the two died first. Both were found murdered, bound and strangled, in their home in 1991. If Michael died first, Susan's heirs would get his estate, because she would therefore have "survived" him (perhaps by mere seconds). If Susan died first, Michael's estate would go to his family.

☞ According to syndicated columnist Jack Anderson, the U.S. Postal Service suffered a courtroom setback in 1992. USPS needed to get an expert-witness list for its side to a Dayton, Ohio, judge by the next day in an employment discrimination case in order to be able to use the witnesses at trial. The list was sent from Washington, D.C., by the Postal Service's overnight Express Mail but did not arrive for ten days.

☞ In 1993, Minneapolis judge Richard Solum dropped prostitution charges against Jacqueline Reina, a.k.a. "Mistress Ayesha," who was found during a police raid in her chambers standing beside a naked client who was strapped to a sawhorse and on whose genitals she had placed sixteen clothespins. Judge Solum reasoned that Reina was not responding to a sexual impulse from the act and therefore could not be guilty of prostitution.

☞ Los Angeles lawyer Gary P. Miller won an $85,000 disability payment from Equitable Life Assurance Society for his claim that he had been allergic to courthouses for two years and therefore could not work at his profession. He claimed that ever since his 1992 arrest on fraud charges, courtrooms cause him stress, mood swings, and physical sickness.

Fetishes on Parade

☞ Pennsylvania district judge Charles O. Guyer was charged in 1991 with improperly favoring a defendant in a case. Police said Guyer privately offered a lenient sentence to a twenty-one-year-old man on the condition that the man allow Guyer to wash his hair. Two undercover police officers set up a sting on Guyer by allowing him to wash their hair, too.

☞ Mark J. Davis, twenty-eight, who was not employed in the dental field, was charged with trying to break into a dentist's office in Aurora, Ohio, in 1992. Police found dental tools and orthodontic devices in his van, and in his home, they found enlarged photographs of girls' mouths as they were undergoing dental work. In Davis's pockets were twenty driver's licenses that had been reported missing—nineteen of them belonging to females who wore, or had worn, braces. Said Aurora police chief Steve Poling, there is "something weird going on here."

☞ In 1992, prominent Easton, Maryland, lawyer George Goldsborough was accused of spanking an employee and clients in his office in incidents going back ten years. An ex-law partner said he found the book *Spanking and the Single Girl* in Goldsborough's desk drawer. (Rumors of other incidents had been circulating around town for years—such that the law firm was referred to locally as Spanky and the Gang.)

☞ Van Patterson, twenty-three, was convicted in 1991 in Painesville, Ohio, of burglary and sex charges as the notorious "BVD bandit" who broke into homes, fondled men as they slept, and cut off their underwear for souvenirs. One man testified that during a fight with his wife one night, she had threatened "to castrate him" and had suggested that he sleep on the sofa. Apparently Mr. Patterson broke into their home during the night and slashed the man's underwear, leaving the man convinced his wife had attempted to carry out her threat until he was informed by coworkers that a "BVD bandit" was on the loose.

The
Concrete
Enema

☞ A Tulsa, Oklahoma, physician, writing in a 1992 issue of the *Irish Journal of Psychological Medicine,* reported on a thirty-two-year-old woman who had become convinced that she was being wooed by Donald Duck. Her neighbors had just installed a large satellite dish, which the woman believed had been placed there to facilitate the "couple's" communication. She spent lots of time "hovering" around the dish and eventually undressed and climbed into it, where she later said she consummated her marriage to Mr. Duck.

☞ Gary Richards, founder of a Jupiter, Florida, company that sells lifelike models of human feet for $74.95 a pair, told the *Palm Beach Post* in 1993 that he sells about 150 pairs a month to the 4,000 or so foot fetishists who subscribe to his catalog/newsletter, *Fantasy Foot News.* As a sideline, women who model their feet for Richards also furnish their used shoes for sale to customers. "Most guys are into the odor," said Richards. "The odor will stay for a long time if you keep the shoe in plastic and then steam it when you want to use it."

☞ A man whose identity was not disclosed in news accounts was arrested in 1993 in Kissimmee, Florida, and charged with misdemeanor lewdness after he tried to obtain the underwear of several police officers to add to his four-hundred-item police underwear collection. When arrested, he was carrying samples of his collection along with videotapes of the TV show *Cops*.

☞ Two California physicians, coauthoring a piece in the March 1993 issue of the *Journal of Forensic Sciences*, reported on the deaths of two men who suffered mishaps while suspended naked on construction vehicles' hydraulic shovels, attempting to heighten sexual gratification. One asphyxiated; the other was accidentally fatally pinned to the ground by the shovel while dressed in women's clothes.

☞ In a 1992 issue of *Sexual and Marital Therapy*, two therapists at the Institute of Psychiatry in London reported "partial" success in "orgasmic reconditioning" of their patient, George, twenty. They got George to switch his masturbatory stimuli from the family car (an Austin Metro) to photographs of naked women.

George had reported arousal previously only when sitting in the car or when squatting behind it while the engine was running.

☞ The *London Independent's* weekly magazine reported in 1993 on the Hush-a-Bye Baby Club in southern England, whose adult male members dress as female infants and refer to themselves as "Baby Michelle," "Baby Cathy," etc. "Mummy Clare" runs the club, charging about $110 a night ($140 for nonmembers), which includes baby food, bottled milk, and diaper service. Spanking is about $7 more per session.

☞ London housewife Julie Amiri, charged in 1993 with shoplifting, sought leniency in court by having her psychologist testify that she is unable to achieve orgasm except from the excitement of a police arrest. Amiri said she had her first orgasm at age twenty-eight in the back of a police car, and the psychologist said that sirens, uniforms, and flashing blue lights were additional turn-ons.

Great Art!

☞ New York artist Rirkrit Tiravanija staged a 1993 show at Chicago's Randolph Street Gallery, consisting of his (1) cooking a Thai meal from scratch for gallery visitors and then (2) leaving the cooking utensils and dirty dishes on display for the next month "as a comment on physical, cultural, and social relationships."

☞ Among the seventy-five works of photographer Joel-Peter Witkin displayed at the Villa Pignatelli in Naples, Italy, in 1993 were "The Kiss" (a photograph of a corpse's head sliced open by a pathologist and joined lip to lip) and "Still Life" (a severed head photographed as a vase containing a flower arrangement).

☞ According to a 1993 story in *New York Newsday,* on permanent display in the living room of a SoHo loft in New York City is 3,600 square feet of dirt, spread two feet thick, titled *Earth Room.* Created in 1980 by conceptual artist Walter DeMaria, *Earth Room,* says curator Bill Dilworth, "has more of an emotional range than the Mona Lisa or the Sistine Chapel."

☞ Canadian sculptor Raymond Mackintosh opened the annual Pennsylvania Farm Show in Harrisburg in 1993 with a nearly life-size statue of a vendor scooping ice cream from a cart for a little boy and girl—but made entirely of butter. And the next month in Chicago, Buddhist monk Sonam Dhargye exhibited several Tibetan yak butter sculptures, each about two feet high, at the Field Museum of Natural History. And the previous summer, Linda Christensen had sculpted "butterheads" out of eighty-five-pound blocks of butter for the Minnesota State Fair.

☞ In late 1992, the French performance artist Orlan completed the fifth episode of plastic surgery, out of a planned seven, in her several-year attempt at art by personal body transformation. She was changing parts of her face and body to conform to Renaissance and post-Renaissance ideals of feminine beauty, and after it's over, an advertising agency will select a new name for her, reflecting the persona that emerges.

☞ As part of sixty-five New York City artists' 1992 "Repohistory" exhibit on various Manhattan street corners, a poster was placed on a lamppost on Maiden Lane (near Wall Street) to explain the origin of the name. Illustrating the poster was a drawing of a female doll wearing typical garb of the late 1700s and carrying laundry in a basket, and an illustration of a hymen taken from a medical textbook. (The two artists responsible for the poster were women.)

☞ According to a 1992 profile in *Advertising Age's Creativity* magazine, Minneapolis artist Judy Olausen had finished nine photographs of a series featuring her seventy-year-old mother portrayed as various objects. Included were her mother kneeling on all fours with a pane of glass on her back ("Mother as Coffee Table") and lying alongside a highway ("Mother as Road Kill"). Olausen said, "My brothers think I'm torturing my mother," but countered that her mother is her best friend: "I'm immortalizing her."

☞ The *Baltimore Sun* reported in 1993 that New York City artist Todd Alden had asked four hundred art collectors worldwide to send him samples of their feces so he can offer them for sale in personalized tins. Said Alden, "Scatology is emerging as an increasingly significant part of artistic inquiry in the 1990s." The feces of Italian artist Piero Manzoni, canned in 1961, sold in the late 1980s for $75,000.

☞ After two years of haggling with a New York art dealer, the National Gallery of Canada announced in 1993 that it had acquired, for $1.5 million, the painting entitled *No. 16,* by American abstract impressionist Mark Rothko. The painting consists merely of two white rectangles on a red background. The asking price was over $4 million.

☞ In 1992 Canadian sculptor Helen Chadwick, thirty-eight, offered her "Piss Flowers" creations—bronze casts of streams of urine—for around $2,000 each. The artist described her work to England's *Guardian*: "I would build a mound of snow with a good density and then urinate in the middle of it. Then I would get a man to encircle my urine [stream] with a stream of his own. The shapes would be like petals with a series of droplets."

She then made a plaster cast of the work, creating a series of twelve flower sculptures.

☞ In 1994 performance artist Ron Athey stunned audience members at the Walker Art Museum in Minneapolis, and caused a national controversy, by slicing the back of accomplice Darryl Carlton onstage, wiping the blood on towels, and passing them on a clothesline over the audience. A Walker spokesperson said Athey had AIDS and that the show was directed at the AIDS-phobic society but that there was no risk to audience members from the infected blood. Carlton said such erotic torture is "revered in Africa and feared in America."

☞ In 1994, the Esbjerg Art Museum in Copenhagen, Denmark, featured an exhibit of six decomposing, beheaded pigs and a mirror covered in pig's blood, in an area twenty-five feet from the museum's restaurant. Said the artist, German sculptor Christian Lemmerz: "This is art that makes people think. They must take a stand on their own existence and face the reality of what happens to their bodies after death." Lemmerz bagged the remains after the exhibit closed and found a collector to buy it.

The Concrete Enema

☞ In 1993, funded in part through a $4,000 grant from the Rockefeller Foundation, three artists selected seventy cows near Boulder, Wyoming, and painted feminist poetry by early settler Phyllis Luman Metal on their hides. Said artist Sue Thornton, "Cows are great, and so are women. Their lives are about self-sacrifice and motherhood."

☞ In 1992, a confused cleaning crew accidentally tossed out an exhibit at the Museum of Discovery and Science in Fort Lauderdale, Florida. The easily mistakable exhibit consisted only of cigarette butts (more than fourteen thousand) crammed into coffee cans.

You Think You've Got a Tough Job

☞ In 1992, Cornell University researcher Ralph Carlton identified the female pheromone of the brown-banded cockroach and went to work immediately on a fungus to suppress it in order to discourage reproduction. Carlton's work involved sifting through the contents of the "sex glands" of fifteen thousand female cockroaches, separating out via a special process the "thousands" of chemicals present in the glands, and finding the one substance that sufficiently neuroelectrically stimulated the male cockroach's antennae.

☞ A 1992 *Austin American-Statesman* story profiled John Stapp, a troubleshooter for the Travis County, Texas, sewage treatment plant, one of the nation's only professional sewage divers. Stapp dons a diving suit, mask, breathing tube, and air-powered tools to perform repairs on the sixty-thousand-gallon, sixteen-foot by forty-foot sewage containment vat. A typical repair job requires Stapp to be submerged for four hours or more, in zero visibility. Stapp describes the job as "very quiet and peaceful" and says that, at the end of a shift, the thing usually on his mind is food: "I'm usually starved when I get through."

☞ Dennis and Pam Ponsness told the Associated Press in 1993 that they often gagged when they opened their maggot farm in Porthill, Idaho, but had recently gotten used to the smell. They raise millions of maggots for bait by putting up to one ton of fish out for the fly larvae to feast on and then refrigerating the maggots until they're ready to ship.

☞ *The Washington Post* reported in 1993 that there are three thousand pet therapists in the United States, including fifty fully certified as animal behaviorists, charging fees of $50 to $135 per hour. Said one therapist, "There's a reason for everything [animals] do." On the other hand, said a skeptical veterinarian, "The pets aren't crazy. The humans are crazy."

☞ The city of Bombay, India, on a cleanup campaign in 1993, announced it had seventy job openings for rat catchers; it received forty thousand applications—half from college graduates.

☞ In New York City in 1992, Donna Goldberg opened Organized Student, a consulting service (at $85 to $125 per hour) that advised children and teenagers on how to clean up their rooms. Said a ninth-grade client interviewed by *The New York Times,* "I try to keep going by myself, but I can't do it."

☞ In 1992, University of California at Berkeley "environmental psychologist" Clare Cooper Marcus started a counseling service for people having difficult relationships with their houses. For $100 an hour, she conducts role-playing sessions between the client and the house. Dr. Marcus says that having the client voice anxieties to the house and having the house "respond" usually begins relieving the client's stress within the first hour.

☞ Dr. Walter H. Kaye, reporting in a 1993 medical journal, found that female bulimics retain around 1,200 calories of food after they purge—no matter how much food they had taken in or what their regurgitation rate was. Kaye and his colleagues came to this conclusion by carefully studying and cataloging the content of the subjects' vomitus.

Inexplicable

☞ Once, in 1992, the U.S. government declined to allow Scotland's "national dish"—haggis—into the country for the January 23 celebrations of the birthday of poet Robert Burns because the food, said officials, was unfit for human consumption. Haggis is minced sheep's heart, lungs, and liver mixed with oatmeal, onions, and black pepper—all boiled in a sheep's stomach until it achieves the uniformly inviting color gray and served with mashed turnips.

☞ *The Philadelphia Inquirer* reported in 1992 on the local "Silent Meeting Club," consisting of several people who gather periodically at various spots around town and make it a point not to speak to each other. Founder John Hudak said his inspiration was seeing how people often feel obligated to talk, even when they really have nothing to say, such as at parties. He was happy "to have a group of people where you wouldn't have to talk."

☞ Moscow, Russia, teenager Vitaly Klimakhin dropped   *Inexplicable*
   out of high school in 1991 to become a writer, according
   to a *Wall Street Journal* article. Over a period of 107 days,
   he turned out a book that consists of only the word
   "Ford" [the automobile] written four hundred thousand
   times. Said Klimakhin, "My work is able to provoke a
   whole range of emotions in people. Some think it is just
   stupid. Others take it a bit more seriously."

☞ In Toronto in 1994, Sajid Rhatti, twenty-three, and his
   twenty-year-old wife brawled over whether Katey Sagal,
   who plays Peg Bundy on the *Married with Children* TV
   show, is prettier than Christina Applegate, who plays her
   daughter. First, the wife slashed Rhatti in the groin with
   a wine bottle as they scuffled, but she dressed his
   wounds, and the couple sat down again to watch another episode of the show. Moments later, the brawl
   erupted again, and Rhatti, who suffered a broken arm
   and shoulder, stabbed his wife in the chest, back, and
   legs before they implored neighbors to call an ambulance.

☞ A Navy Department employee newsletter reported in
   1992 that Bea Perry, a secretary with a navy unit in

Washington, D.C., commutes to work daily from her home in Trenton, New Jersey—171 miles away. She hits the road at 2:30 A.M. to make it to her desk by 6:30 and has been doing it, for several federal agencies in Washington, for twenty-five years.

☞ As President Bush ordered air strikes during his last days in office because of post–Gulf War activities of Saddam Hussein, Patriot missile launchers were set up again in Kuwait—on what are the fairways for the last six holes of the golf course at the Hunting and Equestrian Club in Kuwait City. "I know national security is a priority," golfer Walid Al-Tailji told the Associated Press, "but this [inconvenience to golfers] is another form of invasion."

☞ During the early 1990s, several states' legislators belatedly realized that they had failed to criminalize necrophilia. For example, when Ronald Shawn Ryan, twenty-two, was arrested in 1993 for breaking into an Edmonds, Washington, funeral home on two occasions and having sex with corpses, officials realized they could charge him only with burglary. California, Florida, and Iowa faced similar dilemmas.

☞ Psychology professor Russell Carney of Southwest Missouri State University told the Associated Press in 1992 that he had developed a method for improving memory and told the reporter how he could recall, say, that a particular painting was done by Degas in 1865. First, think of an object that sounds like "Degas" [day-GAH], for example, "dagger," and then memorize the last two digits of the year by learning the sentence "Twin new moons rose low, just clearing four pine saplings," in which the first word begins with a T and stands for "1," the second, N, stands for "2," and so on. Thus, 1865 becomes "65," which becomes "just" "low," which could translate to J-L, which could be "jelly," which would produce a "jelly dagger," to which the subject tries to find a resemblance, somewhere, in the Degas painting. Simple as that.

Inexplicable

☞ A 1993 Associated Press profile of North Carolina State University veterinarian Greg Lewbart reported that he is one of the few in the country who treat pet fish. Dr. Lewbart's fees range from $100 for a checkup, including X rays, to $250 for surgery. He said business is good.

The Concrete Enema

☞ In a 1992 article in the *Journal of Animal Science,* Dr. Steven Loerch reported his finding that inserting a plastic pot scrubber permanently into the top stomach of a cow can satisfy the cow's need for roughage, thus lowering the cost of feeding it.

☞ In 1993, Dorolou Swirsky, eighty-three, told the *San Francisco Chronicle* she would give the city of Sunnyvale, California, $500,000 from her estate to finance youth sports activities, which she viewed as the key antidote to delinquency. She particularly wanted the money to go toward interscholastic lawn bowling, which she said "embraces everything that holds a family together."

☞ *People* magazine reported in 1993 that the Avon cosmetics company had more than thirty-six thousand sales representatives in the Amazonia region of Brazil, with sales growing at 50 percent a year. Photographs showed an expedition by zone manager Sonia Pinheiro to introduce her products to the Tembe Indians in Tenetehara. Avon representatives in Amazonia sell the complete range of Avon products, from lipstick, moisturizer, and mascara to men's bikini briefs, and accept for payment almost any barterable item, such as fish.

☞ In the annual ice-fishing derby in 1994 at the Lake Como Fish and Game Club near Syracuse, New York, Brian Carr beat out three dozen competitors to win, with 155 catches. The temperature that day was minus 30 degrees, and first-prize money was $8.

☞ In court papers submitted in 1993, federal prosecutors accused convicted bank swindler Charles J. Bazarian of a second swindle: He had somehow convinced the district attorney who prosecuted him three years earlier in the Irvine, California, bank swindle to personally invest $6,000 in an Oklahoma company that turned out to be worthless.

Least Meritorious Lawsuits

☞ In Tacoma, Washington, Christine Lauritzen filed a lawsuit against her husband, Bret, in 1991 for subjecting her to injury by his driving. Christine said that if Bret had listened to her and taken the proper turns when she told him to during their visit to Miami, Florida, they wouldn't have wound up in a bad section of town and wouldn't have gotten robbed, and she wouldn't have suffered her arm injury.

☞ Auto mechanic Kenneth Arrowood filed a lawsuit for $2,613 in Cleveland, Ohio, in 1992 against his mother, citing her failure to pay him for fixing her pickup truck. A week later, Hazel Arrowood, seventy-eight, filed a countersuit for her son's ungratefulness, pointing out the many uncompensated services she had provided him over the years as mother, cook, nurse, and bail bondsman, and recommending that the court give Kenneth "the whipping that he so rightly needs and which I failed to give him as a child." (She won the lawsuit, but the judge declined to spank Kenneth.)

☞ In 1992, a New York court threw out a high school student's lawsuit against two classmates. He had sued them for giving him a "flat tire" (stepping on the heel of his shoe), but the judge said the plaintiff failed to show which of the two had actually stepped on it.

☞ During the 1992 presidential campaign, Katherine Balog, sixty, filed a lawsuit in Rancho Cucamonga, California, against Bill Clinton and the Democratic Party to recover damages for the trauma of Clinton's candidacy. The fact that Clinton was then on the verge of becoming president despite allegedly being a "draft dodger" and a "Communist sympathizer" induced in Balog, she said, "serious emotional and mental stress" that was certain to create future medical expenses.

☞ In 1993, the U.S. Court of Appeals in Denver dismissed a lawsuit by convicted police killer Merrill Chamberlain, who had sued the Albuquerque Police Department, claiming that he wouldn't have committed the murder if the officer had been better trained and had prevented him from getting hold of the gun. Also, said Chamberlain, the officer should have been wearing a bulletproof vest, so that when Chamberlain shot him, he would have survived and the penalty wouldn't have been as great.

☞ In 1993, Scott Abrams, twenty-seven, filed a $2 million lawsuit against the owners and managers of an Arlington, Virginia, building for injuries he suffered when he was hit by lightning while sitting on the roof during a severe electrical storm. He said the building owner should have provided signs telling people to stay off the roof during electrical storms.

☞ In 1991 Richard Osborn filed a lawsuit against a Casper, Wyoming, video store for fraud. He said he bought the X-rated *Belle of the Ball* based on a photo on the package featuring actress Busty Belle but later discovered that Belle was onscreen for only nine of the film's sixty-plus minutes. Osborn sought a refund of the $29.95 purchase price, plus $55.79 in reimbursement for medicine because he said the stress of not seeing more of Ms. Belle caused an asthma attack, and $50,000 for pain and suffering.

☞ In 1993, a New York appeals court rejected Edna Hobbs's lawsuit against the company that makes the device called the Clapper. Hobbs claimed she hurt her hands because she had to clap too hard to turn her appliances on: "I couldn't peel potatoes [when my hands hurt]. I never ate so many baked potatoes in my life. I was in pain." However, the judge said Hobbs had merely failed to adjust the sensitivity controls.

☞ Frances Bobnar of Adamsburg, Pennsylvania, filed a lawsuit against the Pennsylvania Lottery Commission in 1994, claiming that she had spent over $150,000 on lottery tickets during the last ten years but had never won.

☞ In 1989, a Union Bridge, Maryland, high school permitted a female, Tawana Hammond, seventeen, to try out for the boys' football team under the pressure of a federal law that prevents gender discrimination. On her first scrimmage, Tawana, a running back, was tackled and suffered massive internal injuries. In 1992, she filed a

*The
Concrete
Enema*

$1.5 million lawsuit against the county board of education for its failure to inform her of how dangerous football is.

☞ In 1992, the Illinois Supreme Court reinstated a $1.5 million verdict against the Chicago Transit Authority in a 1977 wrongful death lawsuit. The family of Korean immigrant Sang Yeul Lee had sued CTA after Sang, who was drunk, was electrocuted as he urinated on the "third rail."

Delicious

☞ The venerable San Francisco watchdog organization, Consumer Action, which usually issues advisories on more-mainstream product and service frauds, warned consumers in 1992 that adult "900" telephone services often promise more explicit sexual conversation than they deliver: "Despite highly suggestive titles and pictures of half-naked women in many ads," wrote an alarmed Consumer Action, "the services provided tame, nonsexual conversation."

☞ John Hurst was taken to a mental health center after he was discovered, disoriented, propping a ladder up to the second floor of the Kennedy family estate in Palm Beach in 1991. However, it wasn't clear that he was really disoriented; he told police when they arrived, "I'm looking for my wife. I think she may be up there."

☞ Billy Milligan, thirty-seven, was hired in 1992 to direct a $3 million film based on the life of a serial rapist who

plagued Columbus, Ohio, in the late 1970s and who is
now in prison. Milligan had never directed before; his
only qualification for the job was that he was a serial
rapist, himself, in the 1970s. He had apparently im-
pressed Hollywood director James Cameron during the
shooting of Milligan's own life story, *The Crowded Room.*

☞ Polly, a Plainview, Minnesota, cow, had predicted the
winner of each presidential election from 1972 to 1988
by relieving herself upon a photograph of the eventual
winner after equal numbers of the candidates' photographs were spread on the ground. The day before
the 1992 election, after ten photos each of Clinton,
Bush, and Perot were spread out in a pen in a shopping
mall parking lot, Polly's celebrated patty landed squarely
on a photograph of Bill Clinton.

☞ In 1975, the Federal Communications Commission rejected a request from two citizens to investigate religious
broadcasters' alleged abuses of reserved "educational"
radio channels, but the rumor persisted that the FCC
was about to kick religious stations off the air altogether.
By December 1992, the FCC had received more than

twenty-one million letters from parishioners urging it   *Delicious*
not to grant the 1975 petition. The FCC issues an
annual admonition that the public disregard the rumor,
but letters continue to flood the agency.

☞ With many of its leaders still in jail from their 1980s'
fund-raising scheme of choice—robbing armored cars—
the white supremacist group Aryan Nations began
a new fund-raising operation in 1991. The group sold
mail-order candies to a private membership list through
a Hayden, Idaho, firm, Intermountain FARE. The best-
selling selection, for $8.50 plus postage and handling,
is the Royal Nut Mix.

☞ In 1992 retired Dallas, Texas, police officer James
Leavelle, who was the man in the white hat handcuffed
to Lee Harvey Oswald at the moment Jack Ruby shot
Oswald in 1963, was in his home re-creating for news-
man Bob Porter just how he had grabbed Ruby's gun to
prevent a second shot at Oswald. Using the same model
gun Ruby had used, while Porter's camera was rolling as
part of his project on the history of the Kennedy assassi-
nation, Leavelle accidentally shot Porter in the arm,

sending him to Parkland Hospital, just like Kennedy and Oswald. Porter, however, survived.

☞ Among the abstract watercolors chosen by the Manchester (England) Academy of Fine Arts for its prestigious annual show in 1993 was *Rhythm of the Trees,* whose "certain quality of color balance, composition, and technical skill," said the judges, earned its place among the works selected from the 1,000 submitted. The painting, composed of random color smudges, was done by four-year-old Carly Johnson and submitted by her mother as a joke.

☞ Alvin Lastimado, Jr., eighteen, was arrested in 1992 in Wahiawa, Hawaii, and charged with assault. He had been holding a woman against her will in his home, where he began to utter a satanic chant. In the middle of the chant, he forgot the words and told the woman he had to go to the public library to look them up. The woman got free and called the police, who intercepted Lastimado in the "occult" section.

☞ In 1992 in Troy, New York, Todd W. Bariteau, Sr., thirty-two, pleaded guilty to robbing, for the second time, a boutique called Déjà Vu.

☞ In 1993, Mark Kreider of New Castle, Delaware, a full-time Grateful Dead concert attender ("Deadhead"), was robbed of $5 and shot in the back in a mugging following a Dead concert in Sacramento, California. Kreider could not supply police with details of the crime because he said he did not realize he had been shot until about an hour afterward. Four months later, Christopher Swihart, twenty, was arrested in Berkeley, California, after breaking into a house and taking a suitcase. Swihart told police he didn't know where he was, that he thought the suitcase was his, and that the last thing he remembered doing was attending a Grateful Dead concert the night before.

☞ In 1993 near Alvin, Texas, Andrea Guerero, eighteen, and her brother came across a man who was slumped over his truck and not breathing, and Andrea saved his life by administering CPR until an ambulance arrived.

Delicious

At the time, Guerero was on her way home from a CPR certification exam, which she had flunked.

☞ According to a U.S. Department of Energy memo reported by *The Denver Post* in 1992, the number of workers it takes to change a light bulb, on a certain safety system at the Rocky Flats nuclear weapons plant, is forty-three, requiring 1,087.1 person-hours.

☞ The epicenter of the January 1994 California earthquake was five miles from the United States' largest egg farm, where hens had produced their usual one million eggs in the hours before the quake hit. The damage to the farm was a snapped water line, toppled empty egg pallets, and a total of one broken egg. Said manager Robert Wagner to his employees, "We had a 6.6 earthquake that broke less than you guys do when we're working."

☞ Camden, North Carolina, sculptor Maria Juliana Kirby-Smith offered for sale in 1992 a three-foot-high lawn jockey statue of U.S. senator Strom Thurmond, for $700.

Schemes

☞ Authorities in Bangkok arrested Brazilian Julio Cesar de Monraes Barros in 1991 for shoplifting diamonds from a jewelry store. Barros had surgically implanted a suction tube in the little finger of his left hand, running along his arm to a collection device under his armpit, from which $12,000 worth of diamonds was recovered.

☞ Charges were filed against Mineola, New York, plumber Joseph Conretta, thirty-one, in 1992 for an idea he carried out in a women's rest room at Nassau Community College. Conretta had prepared a low-rise wooden box that appeared to be a platform and placed it on the floor so that women using the sinks and mirrors would have to stand on it. Unknown to them, Conretta was lying inside the box, peering up their skirts through a peephole.

☞ Over the past six years, at least five women and girls have been arrested on various charges related to their bandaging down their breasts and dressing as males in order to seduce women and girls for sex. For example, in 1992, Shana Fuller, twenty-one, from a Houston, Texas, suburb, was given five years' probation for offenses involving a sixteen-year-old girl whom she dated for a year. Said the mother of the girl, "She [Fuller] is an attractive girl, but she also was an attractive guy."

☞ The Jerusalem News Service reported in 1993 that chemist Rabbi Moshe Antelman had invented a bullet that he believed would do more than merely kill Islamic fundamentalist terrorists physically. The bullets contain small amounts of pork; many Muslims believe that any contact whatsoever with swine will kill their souls.

☞ Mikhail Maley, defense adviser to Russian president Boris Yeltsin, proposed in 1992 that emergency relief food and supplies be lobbed to remote areas of the world in SS-18 intercontinental ballistic missiles. *Aviation Week and Space Technology* reported Maley's suggestion that six or seven tons of supplies would fit where the nuclear warheads had been housed.

☞ In 1992, New Orleans police arrested Donald Simmons, *Schemes*
fifty-three, and Cheryl Collins, thirty-eight, for breaking
into parking meters. Police said the two would walk
along a street and passionately embrace every few yards,
but that that was a ruse. In reality, they would embrace
around a parking meter, and Simmons would open it
with a key and slip the money to Collins, who would
put it into a bag under her skirt—all in about twelve
seconds' time. A police officer said Simmons admitted
to having practiced the scheme since 1985.

☞ The local board of health closed down the Wing Wah
Chinese restaurant in South Dennis, Massachusetts,
briefly in 1992 for various violations. The most serious,
said officials, was the restaurant's practice of draining
water from cabbage by putting it in cloth laundry bags,
placing them between two pieces of plywood in the
parking lot, and driving over them with a van. Said
health director Ted Dumas, "I've seen everything now."

☞ In 1993, Pittsburgh, Pennsylvania, police sought a
drifter, Elmore Ray Harvey, in connection with the theft
of 4,220 quarters from a money-changing machine in a

Laundromat over a two-month period. Allegedly, Harvey inserted a one-dollar bill (to which he had tied a string) into the machine until just the proper moment when the quarters were dispatched, then pulled it back out. An even trickier string scheme was reported by Malaysia's *New Straits Times* in 1994: A man in Perak, Malaysia, was arrested after several incidents in which he had climbed on roofs at night and, using a fishing line and hook, lifted the sarongs of sleeping women to look at their bodies.

☞ According to the *Jerusalem Report* newspaper, Israeli Danny Abu, forty-three, wandered around a Palestinian village for several hours on April 19, 1993, because he was suicidally despondent and hoped he would become the target of a terrorist attack. Still alive after several hours, he went into a shop in the village of Dir al-Utzon and asked specifically that local representatives of the Black September terrorists be summoned to attack him.

☞ George W. Smith, a Bill Clinton supporter, told the *Arkansas Democrat-Gazette* in 1994 of his plan to help with one of the president's Whitewater problems. To reduce potential taxpayer liability for the failure of the Madison Guaranty Savings and Loan, Smith would encourage private contributions toward the bailout—by rebating baseball trading cards to each contributor from Smith's four-room collection, at $2 in card value for each $1 contributed. Smith thought $2 million could be raised toward the projected bailout cost of $47 million.

Latest Religious Messages

☞ Rev. Glen Summerford was convicted in 1992 of the attempted murder of his wife in Scottsboro, Alabama. A jury found that he had forced his wife to stick her hand into a cage of rattlesnakes (which he handles in his services at his "Church of Jesus with Following Signs"—in addition to drinking strychnine and touching live electrical wires), saying that she had to die because he wanted to marry another woman. (And while Summerford was in jail, his inadequately supervised parishioner, Clyde Crossfield, was bitten on both hands by a rattlesnake he was handling.)

☞ Rev. Edward Mullen of St. Edward Catholic Church in Providence, Rhode Island, who believes the U.S. Supreme Court is too strict on the separation of church and state, said in 1992 that he would no longer permit parishioners to pray for government officials in his church.

☞ In a deposition made public in 1992 in an Albuquerque sexual abuse lawsuit, Catholic priest Robert Kirsch admitted that he had had sexual intercourse with a woman but denied that the action had violated his vow of chastity. He was merely engaging in a "reserved embrace," which he said was sexual intercourse with "no passion, no kissing, no [ejaculation]," and which he said is not improper under Catholic theology.

☞ In 1993, Israel's national telephone company initiated a fax service that transmits messages to God via the Wailing Wall in Jerusalem. And the same year, the Roman Catholic Church unveiled a high-tech confessional that accepts confessions by fax. Also in 1993, a sect of Orthodox Jews in Brooklyn, New York, began selling its members special beepers so they would know instantly when the Messiah arrives on Earth.

☞ In 1994 in New Orleans, a fleeing bank robber fired several shots at a police officer but hit a nearby thirty-eight-year-old nun from the Sisters Servants of Mary Convent. The nun's wound was slight because the prayer book she was carrying absorbed most of the bullet's impact.

☞ Police in Chandler, Arizona, said that Wilputte Alanson Sherwood, a priest who was arrested in 1993 and charged with sex crimes against teenage boys, kept videotapes and meticulous logs of his adventures. Police learned, for instance, that since 1984, Father Sherwood had picked up exactly 3,908 men and boys along local freeways (a rate of at least 1.18 per day) and taken 1,840 of them to his home to have sex with.

☞ Four families in Burlington County, New Jersey, filed a lawsuit against the Catholic Church in 1993, claiming damages for emotional distress caused by the church's failure to remove a priest whom they reported had sexually abused their children three years earlier. The couples claim that, as a result of the priest's staying on at the St. Mary of the Lakes Church in Medford, New Jersey, they lost their faith and thus stand a lesser chance of getting into heaven.

☞ One of the familiar landmarks of Topeka, Kansas, in the last few years has been the picketing of funerals of gay men staged by Baptist preacher Fred Phelps. (He uses signs such as "God Hates Fags: Romans 9:13.") In 1993, Phelps admitted he had made up and spread a rumor that a Topeka city council member had AIDS.

☞ The Toronto *Globe and Mail* reported in 1993 on the religious importance of Pepsi-Cola in the town of San Juan Chamula in southern Mexico. Practicing a blend of Christianity and the worship of Mayan gods, many parishioners believe their leaders' doctrine that because Pepsi has more bubbles than Coca-Cola, it is closer to the Sun and thus more powerful. Bottles of Pepsi appear among holy artifacts inside local churches, and some leaders believe the cola has healing powers. (Coca-Cola officials say the dominance is due purely to Pepsi's payment of kickbacks to the leaders.)

Frontiers of Science

☞ To help speed up the breeding of fleas for laboratory use to study human and animal allergies, researchers at Cornell University in 1992 patented an artificial dog for the fleas to nest on. Previously, the lab had required twenty-five flea-infested dogs to breed the twelve thousand fleas per day needed.

☞ United States Department of Agriculture scientists announced in 1992 that pumping cottage cheese whey onto sloping fields could cut soil erosion 65 percent to 75 percent. It was the whey's milky stickiness that made it effective.

☞ In 1992, biologists at China's Northwest University reported finding a seventy-seven-pound slimeball floating on a river in Shaanxi Province. According to the scientists, the white fungus gained twenty-two pounds in the first three days the scientists observed it, and had the ability to move across the ground on its own.

☞ Writing in a 1992 medical journal, two doctors in Bristol, England, reported the case of a fifty-three-year-old man who came to a hospital emergency room, "alert and oriented," but with two holes in his skull—the result of a suicide attempt with an electric drill. The doctors' literature search on "deliberate self-harm" by "craniocerebral penetrat[ion]" produced reports of incidents with nails (four reports), ice picks (two), keys (five), pencils (three), and chopsticks (six). In 1993, in a response to that article, five Phoenix, Arizona, physicians reported the case of a thirty-four-year-old man who manually forced a ballpoint pen through his right eye in an apparent suicide attempt so that only about one inch of it was sticking out of the socket.

☞ Reuters news service reported in 1993 that a seventy-two-year-old retired gardener in England had been credited with self-diagnosis of a tear in his bladder. The man tested his theory of what he had by urinating into a plant pot; eventually a tomato plant sprouted. Doctors said that that indicated a leakage—in this case, of microscopic tomato seeds—between his bowel and his bladder. Doctors said growing urine cultures is the ordinary

way of detecting such a tear but that this was the first
self-diagnosis they had heard of.

☞ A 1993 *Boston Globe* story on the Soiree strip joint in
South Boston disclosed that dancer Taylor Monet, thirty-
three, believed she had the world's first inflatable breasts,
the result of a "valve and hose" implantation that allowed her to inject or extract a saline solution to vary
the size of her silicone breasts between a minimum
40-D and a maximum 96.

☞ A veterinarian in Berwick-Upon-Tweed, England, told
the Associated Press in 1994 that the cause of attrition
among swans on the River Tweed is recent clean-water
rules. Dr. David Rollo said the swans' main food—
effluent from the decaying of barley—is no longer
abundant in the river. And the U.S. Environmental
Protection Agency in 1993 ordered the city of San Diego,
California, to stop its cleanup of a portion of the Tijuana
River because the efforts would cause irreparable harm
to the "sewage-based ecology."

Government in Action

☞ Lynne F. Herron, thirty-three, was hired in 1991 as a municipal bus driver in Cleveland, Ohio, by the Regional Transit Authority. She had just been fired as a municipal train driver after an accident that injured fourteen people, which she caused by deliberately disengaging a safety system. The city's labor contract at the time required that anyone fired because of a train accident be rehired immediately as a bus driver.

☞ Among the information that came to light in 1992 as a result of Atlanta's then-new municipal financial disclosure law was news of the city's obscure "Board of Astrology." The Associated Press could find no records of the board at city hall but concluded after interviews that its three members administer tests to prospective astrologers to make sure they are "qualified."

☞ The *Daily Oklahoman* reported in 1992 that a state-run juvenile counseling center in Tecumseh, Oklahoma, with only thirteen clients, had seventy-two full-time employees and eighteen other professionals on contract.

☞ At a 1992 public meeting of Los Angeles County government's fourteen-member Ritual Abuse Task Force, several members renewed their claims that satanic forces were spraying a pesticide into their offices, homes, and cars in order to prevent them from investigating human sacrifice, torture, and sex orgies. One member said she was poisoned through the vents during a task force meeting in the Los Angeles Hall of Administration. Said the county's chief of toxic epidemiology, who was in attendance, "I can't believe I'm sitting here listening to this."

☞ The Pryor, Oklahoma, *Daily Times* reported in 1992 that autopsies on a minnow and a flea, which the city used to test the quality of discharge from its waste-treatment plant, would cost the city at least $100,000. Tests are required by the state and federal governments to ascertain whether the minnow and the flea died from natural causes or from a problem with the discharge.

☞ The *Los Angeles Times* reported in 1993 that, in order to meet state-mandated quotas for low-income housing in each city, three affluent towns near Los Angeles would begin including in their housing totals the servants' quarters on large estates.

☞ In 1994, Philadelphia's Department of Licenses and Inspections served notice of a violation on dancer Crystal Storm at the Doll House. The Department's weights and measures division, whose primary job is checking the accuracy of meat-market scales, ascertained Ms. Storm's bust measurement at only 50 inches, versus her advertised measurement of "127," which Ms. Storm said was in centimeters. Said department official Frank Antico, "That's deceptive advertising."

☞ The Los Angeles *Daily News* reported in 1994 that the city's Department of Building and Safety had ordered an adult nightclub to remove its stage, which was built to resemble a large shower where nude dancers would cavort for customers' enjoyment. Authorities said the shower was not wheelchair-accessible for disabled nude dancers, although no such dancers had ever come forward.

☞ On March 8, 1994, the New York City Division of School Facilities finally attached doors to the stalls in the girls' rest room at P.S. 206 in Brooklyn, following years of complaining by the principal. The doors were requisitioned on May 25, 1989—1,747 days earlier.

☞ Vice President Al Gore's national performance review of federal government practices revealed in 1994 that the Pentagon spent $4.3 billion a year on travel— $2.0 billion for the travel itself and $2.3 billion to process the paperwork.

☞ A bill introduced in the Georgia legislature in 1994 by representative Doug Teper of Atlanta would have required warnings in all hotel rooms that fornication, adultery, and sodomy are illegal in the state. The bill also requires that the warnings be in Braille and "internationally recognized symbols" (which were not specified in the bill).

☞ In 1992, the selectmen (town council) of Salem, New Hampshire, reluctantly renewed the contract of city manager Barry Brenner for a year, provided that he cleans off his desk. According to one of the selectmen, Brenner had such huge piles of papers that he refuses to let people see his office and in fact earlier in 1992 misplaced town check vouchers and could not find them for six months.

☞ According to long-secret documents obtained in 1992 by the Canadian Press news agency, police in Ottawa had tried during the 1960s to identify every single gay man in Ontario and to prove their findings with a box they called the "fruit machine." Men were shown the box, containing erotic photos, and measurements were taken of the man's pupil size, palm sweat, and blood flow in order to tell whether he had become excited. Files were opened on 8,200 men, and 395 were eventually kicked out of government jobs.

Just Plain Silly

☞ In 1991, the Avon, Colorado, town council resorted to a contest to name the new Eagle River bridge linking I-70 with Highway 6. Sifting through eighty-four suggestions (such as "Eagle Crossing"), the council voted, 4–2, to name the bridge "Bob."

☞ In 1991, Michigan state trooper Fred Sweeney chased a speeder doing 101 mph. After he came upon the man's abandoned car on a side road, Sweeney saw a nearby field of tall grass and noticed that all the cows seemed to be clustered, staring at a particular spot on the ground. Sweeney approached the cows and arrested the speeder.

☞ The government of Ukraine sponsored a competition in 1992 to determine the best way seal off the destroyed nuclear reactor that caused the disaster at Chernobyl in 1986. The government sought a solution that would guarantee safety from radiation for one hundred years and was willing to pay whoever designed such a system top dollar—about $20,000. (The real cost of such a safe design, according to U.S. officials, is well over $250 million.)

☞ In 1992 the cable TV company that serves Columbia, South Carolina, aimed a camera full-time at an aquarium to fill up a vacant channel, which had been reserved for the imminent start-up of the Science-Fiction Channel. When Sci-Fi replaced the "fish channel," complaints were so numerous that the company was forced to find another channel for the aquarium, which was reinstated for a fourteen-hour run every day, sharing time with the Bravo Channel.

☞ Randall Eugene Davis, who has only one leg, was arrested in Clarinda, Iowa, in 1992, suspected of stealing a truck. In the back of the truck at the time of the theft was the owner's Labrador retriever, which had only three legs.

☞ Larry Burchfield, twenty-eight, was arrested in Martins-ville, Indiana, in 1992 and charged with burglary. He was discovered inside a home at 3 A.M. when the owners were awakened by the sound of Burchfield playing their piano. He said he had been overcome by the urge to play and did not stop until police arrived.

☞ In 1993 a truck driver, Hari Singh, hijacked an Airbus airliner over India, claiming to have explosives wired to his body and protesting political corruption and the fighting between Hindus and Muslims in India. Eight hours later, on the ground in Amristar, India, after sev-eral attempts to divert the 192-passenger flight, Singh announced he was giving up the hijacking, whereupon dozens of passengers rushed toward him to get his auto-graph before the authorities could apprehend him.

☞ South African KwaZulu leader Mangosuthu Buthelezi began his 1993 state-of-the-state policy address to the KwaZulu legislature on March 12, spoke continuously during weekday business hours, and finished on March 30—reading 427 pages of text and waiting for the trans-lation from English to Zulu.

☞ In 1993, Baron Trevor, sixty-four, a member of the British House of Lords since 1950, took to the floor to make his very first speech to that body, saying that after forty-three years he had finally found an issue "that affected the locality in which I live." He spoke on the need not to oversupervise police officers.

☞ Among the projects cited in a 1994 *Denver Post* article on the ten "worst ideas in modern U.S. environmental history": a plan by a Department of the Interior official in the 1960s to flood the Grand Canyon for a hydroelectric plant; a plan by then–Atomic Energy Commission chairman James Schlesinger to dispose of nuclear waste by shooting it into the Sun on a space shuttle; and the World Health Organization's 1960s program to kill mosquitoes on Borneo with U.S.-made DDT, which so disrupted the food chain that the island was soon overrun with rats, until the United States parachuted in cats to control them.

Death

☞ Bobby Joe Reid died in 1991 in Taylors, South Carolina, of a seizure and cerebral hemorrhage while having sex with his married girlfriend on the floor of her living room. To cover up the tryst, the frightened woman dragged Reid into her backyard and called police to report a prowler. However, the woman was obviously frazzled: Reid's pants were still around his ankles when police arrived.

☞ In 1992 Marc Cienkowski, twenty-six, confessed to the murder of his friend, Michael Klucznik, thirty-one, in Doylestown Borough, Pennsylvania, after a dispute over a game of Monopoly. Cienkowski shot Klucznik through the heart with a bow and arrow because, according to the district attorney, "[Cienkowski] wanted to be the car rather than the thimble or the hat."

☞ In 1992 a twenty-nine-year-old man from Moab, Utah, fell to his death off the North Rim of the Grand Canyon while backing up to have his picture taken.

☞ It may be an occupational hazard for stand-up comedians to "die" onstage, but in Tempe, Arizona, a comedian who worked as "Joe Michaels" actually died, of a heart aneurysm, during a 1992 performance. He was emceeing a version of *The Dating Game* at Rowdy's Bar when he said, "Bachelor Number One," then collapsed and fell off the stage.

☞ David Wayne Godin, twenty-two, drowned near Dartmouth, Nova Scotia, in 1992 as he was returning from his bachelor stag party and his vehicle plunged into a lake. Attached to Godin's leg, courtesy of his friends at the party, was an authentic ball and chain.

☞ In 1993, Army Corps of Engineers employee Thomas Iracki, thirty-six, leaped to his death in downtown San Francisco after telling several colleagues that he had become despondent at the Clinton administration's "reinventing government" budget cuts to his agency.

The Concrete Enema

☞ In Commerce City, Colorado, in 1993, a thirty-nine-year-old man riding a motorcycle on U.S. 85 was killed when a forty-pound dog fell off an overhead railroad bridge on top of him, causing him to lose control of the cycle and collide with a truck.

☞ Authorities in Hauppauge, New York, said in 1994 that Scott McCraw, thirty-seven, probably committed suicide after an argument with his ex-girlfriend. McCraw's body was found alongside the frozen remains of his pet rattlesnake, and officials believe McCraw took his life by letting the snake bite him numerous times.

☞ According to a note in a 1993 medical journal, *The Lancet*, a man attempting suicide in England was rescued after he had spent more than an hour inhaling automobile exhaust fumes. Doctors attributed his survival to the new catalytic-converter standards in the European Community.

Japan

☞ Japan Efficiency Headquarters, an "entertainment business company" in Chiba, Japan, rents "family members" out to senior citizens who live alone but would like the benefits of a close-knit family from time to time. Typically a husband, wife, and child are requested, and have been trained by the company to engage in family-type activities as if everyone in the room were related. The typical cost for the three family members for three hours is $1,100.

☞ In Japan, where Americans have long complained of the closed retail distribution system for their products, U.S. and Australian beef importers have begun to bypass stores and sell cuts of meat in vending machines for about $12 a pound. In fact, vending machines are much more a part of commerce in Japan than in the United States. Ubiquitous Japanese vending machines routinely dispense, among other things, roses, pearls, beer, pornographic comics, condoms, servings of rice, dried squid snacks, noodle soup, and binoculars. In 1993, police in Chiba, Japan, announced the arrests of three men for selling schoolgirls' used underpants in vending machines at a price of about $30 for a set of three. (The men were accused of violating the Antique Dealings Act, which regulates the sales of used goods.)

☞ Japan's labor department ruled in 1993 against the claim of Yuji Iguchi, who had filed for compensation arguing that her husband's recent death at age forty-three was due to his having worked 360 straight days at a supermarket just before he died. The government said the work record did not qualify as excessive.

☞ The Environmental Assessment Center in Okayama, Japan, announced in 1993 that it had manufactured an experimental sausage out of recycled Tokyo sewage by adding soybean protein and steak flavoring to "sewage solids." A company spokesman said, "[S]ewage isn't really such a dangerous and dirty thing." However, he did not foresee commercially marketing the sausage: "Sewage does have a slight image problem. I don't

think people will be content eating something they *Japan*
know has been excreted by humans."

☞ A pro–nuclear power video, created in 1993 by a private
company seeking to develop nuclear reactors in Japan,
featured the cartoon character "Mr. Pluto," who down-
played the risks of plutonium to the primarily school-
age audiences. Said Mr. Pluto, "If everyone treats me
with a peaceful and warm heart, I'll never be scary or
dangerous." A narrator said plutonium is so safe that if
a person drank it, most of it would pass through his
body without harm.

☞ In 1993, *The Economist* reported that Japan's meteorol-
ogy agency had recently completed a seven-year study
to ascertain the validity of the Japanese legend that
earthquakes are caused by catfish wiggling their tails.
After trying to match catfish tail-wagging with a number
of small earthquakes, the agency abandoned the study,
refusing to confirm or dispute the legend.

☞ In a 1993 report, *The New York Times* described New
Year's Eve on a mountain near Ashikaga, fifty miles

The Concrete Enema

north of Tokyo, in which participants in an annual festival walk in darkness to a temple while expressing themselves vocally in ways never permitted by their polite society. They scream obscenities and indecencies, aimed at politicians or supervisors ("My teacher is an idiot!" "Give me a raise!"). Women, also, are permitted this rare opportunity to use abusive language.

Loners

☞ Joan Abery, seventy, passed away in Reading, England, in 1992 after having lived entirely in the garden outside her house for the previous thirty-five years. She moved there, among twigs, umbrellas, and car seats, after being spurned at the altar—so that she could leave her house in the same condition it was at the time she was jilted.

☞ Agence France-Presse reported in 1992 that Michael Balama, forty-five, a farmer and father of nine children, had resurfaced, living in a tree in Pankshin, Nigeria, after having disappeared two weeks earlier from a nearby tree in which he had been living for five years. He said he wanted to come down but couldn't because "some people are holding me." Balama's wife said, "What I miss about Michael is that we can no longer make love together and produce more children."

☞ Relatives of Dargan Suther, who died in 1990, fought for several years afterward over an estate worth more than $600,000. Before his death at age seventy-three, Suther had taken to living in a tent in his yard in Birmingham, Alabama, because his house was so filled with possessions, mostly decades-old newspapers, that it was impossible to walk through it.

☞ Library officials in Sidney, British Columbia, reported that a "mystery editor" was stalking the library in 1992, compulsively "correcting" text of which he disapproved. For example, long notes handwritten in margins of books explained why "the British Isles" is not the same thing as "Great Britain."

☞ The Associated Press reported in 1993 that Ernest Dittemore had completed eighteen years of sleeping in a four-foot by ten-foot hole in the ground on his property in Troy, Kansas. When Dittemore's house burned down in 1978, he began to spend nights in the hole, and when neighbors chipped in to buy him a trailer to live in, he moved his possessions into it but continued to spend nights in the hole, which he says is "a lot easier to heat."

☞ In 1992, a court in Oslo, Norway, ruled that Oslo University did not have to readmit a current student, a thirty-nine-year-old astrophysics major, until he bathed. The man had been living in a cave near the campus for fourteen years and had sued the university for $470,000 for denying him access to an exam. He said the case was about "my right to decide how I want to live" and "not about whether I smell bad or not," but the court said it was the latter.

☞ Retired Mongolian physician Ichinnorof Dendev, sixty, and two countrymen took a nine-month "walk" in 1993 from Mongolia to Seattle, Washington, in order to place flowers on the grave of the late martial arts star Bruce Lee, who apparently was very popular in Mongolia.

☞ In 1994, the New Hope, Minnesota, home of a forty-four-year-old woman was condemned by health authorities acting on neighbors' complaints. They removed 454 live rats and estimated that another five hundred were hiding in the walls. Authorities found a bed completely covered with nesting rats and said much of the furniture, walls, and about one hundred oil paintings in the basement nad been gnawed through. It all started, the woman said, with three rats she bought as food for her snake.

☞ In 1993, Susumu Suzuki, forty-five, was arrested in Takasaki, Japan, and charged with having made approximately 8,500 phone calls to city hall—as many as several hundred a day—and then hanging up without speaking. He cited as his motive a twenty-year-old snub by city hall when he applied for a job after graduating from college. Two months later, Mikiko Miyamoto, forty-three, was charged with having made as many as one hundred similar phone calls a day for twelve years to a female acquaintance in Tokyo.

☞ A thirty-one-year-old man turned himself in to Anchorage, Alaska, police in 1992, claiming to be the fugitive who had been appearing at local day-care centers in diapers and trying to get them to take him in. Two years before, "Dr. Diaper" (as the local media dubbed him) had contracted with a baby-sitter by phone, claiming to be the parent of an abnormally large eighteen-year-old boy who had the mentality of a toddler, who needed to be changed and fed, and whose bad habits (masturbating in public) should be ignored. When the baby-sitter arrived, the giant baby was, of course, Dr. Diaper himself. On another occasion, a prospective baby-sitter said Dr. Diaper had come to her door once carrying his own three-year-old son because he could not find a real baby-sitter for the boy while he went out on his escapade.

The Continuing Crisis

☞ Rock music sculptress Cynthia Plaster Caster (who creates plaster-of-paris models of rock stars' penises) battled music mogul Herb Cohen in the early 1990s over ownership of twenty-five of her gems, including Jimi Hendrix's. In May 1992, several bands in Chicago staged a benefit concert ("Hard Aid") to help with her legal fees.

☞ The traveling Jim Rose Circus has several noteworthy acts, including the nerve-racking Mr. Lifto, who pulls cement blocks off the ground using small chains attached to his nipple rings. In 1993, Jim Rose himself was forced to postpone a thirty-three-city tour for one month while he recuperated from a Netherlands show in which he yielded to TV and radio stations' requests and ate five lightbulbs in one day (versus his usual limit of no more than one every twenty-four hours). He was laid up with stomach cramps and bleeding bowels.

☞ In Grand Junction, Colorado, in 1993, firefighters called to a potential suicide scene were successful in talking a forty-two-year-old man down from the courthouse roof, but they made backup preparations in case their negotiations failed by borrowing a huge, inflatable hamburger from a nearby Burger King to break the man's fall.

☞ In 1993, an Iowa administrative law judge ruled that former dishwasher Tom Schneckloth had "good cause" for quitting his job at a restaurant in Glenwood, Iowa, and was thus entitled to unemployment benefits. Schneckloth's quitting was understandable, the judge said, because the restaurant's owners, Kathy and Dan Smith, often had marital fights in the kitchen and would sometimes throw knives at each other.

☞ For its 1992 grand opening in Bartlett, Tennessee, Dyer's Café brought in cooked grease its owners said was eighty years old, transported from Dyer's flagship hamburger restaurant in Memphis by sheriff's deputies on motorcycles. Said owner Jim Marshall, "The grease is our secret, and it's got to be protected."

☞ Brazil endured a scandal in 1994 over the appearance of a topless model (who had donned a minidress for the occasion) in the president's box along a parade route during the country's annual Carnival. President Itamar Franco, sixty-three, held hands with Lilian Ramos, twenty-seven, and occasionally kissed her. Photos of the couple showed clearly that Ramos, frequently raising her arms to wave to the parade, was not wearing underpants. Responding to the subsequent criticism, Franco told reporters, "How am I supposed to know if people are wearing underwear?"

☞ McDonnell Douglas Corp., needing to demonstrate that up to 410 passengers could be safely evacuated from its MD-11 jetliner, conducted two tests in 1991 in Los Angeles. Although eleven passengers were injured in the first test, the company proceeded with the second test, which injured thirty-six more people, including one sixty-year-old woman who suffered a broken spine and is now paralyzed from the neck down. Though most of the victims were McDonnell Douglas employees, the paralyzed woman was recruited from a senior citizens' organization (at $49 a head) to comply with the federal requirement that 15 percent of the test passengers be over age fifty. A company spokesman said the number of injuries was "well within the FAA and company expectations."

☞ An organization of several dozen men met regularly in the San Francisco area in 1991 to discuss ways to restore their foreskins, according to a story in the *San Jose Mercury News*. RECAP ("Recover a Penis") members were divided as to technique between surgical reconstruction and "stretching," described by founder Wayne Griffiths as pulling loose skin over his penis and taping it in place using "Foreballs," a device he invented, consisting of two small ball bearings that add weight to pull the skin down. Griffiths said he wore the device for up to twelve hours a day, five days a week, for a year, which gave him enough skin to cover the head of his penis without taping. "The [sexual] feelings are sensational," he said. Said a urologist who supports the group, "They want to enhance their image whether it is in their pants or on their face. Who am I to say otherwise?"

☞ In 1992 in a New York City supermarket, according to a New York *Daily News* story, one customer became upset that another had more than ten items at an express checkout line and precipitated a loud argument, which culminated with the angry woman shouting at the checkout-abuser, "I spit into your groceries." Unfortunately for the woman, the alleged checkout-abuser was the wife of reputed mobster John Gotti. Victoria Gotti said she "used connections" to trace the woman's license plate, went to the woman's home, and dumped a box of dog feces on her.

☞ In 1991, University of Tennessee football player Tom Myslinski attracted much press attention with his pregame ritual: blasting heavy-metal music on his boombox, banging his unhelmeted head "hard" against a shower room wall, and, not surprisingly, "serious" (according to a teammate) vomiting. "I don't know why I do it," said Myslinski. "It's really stupid when you think about it."

☞ In 1992, Natalie Pollock, candidate for mayor of Winnipeg, Manitoba, brawled with a professional

stripper on the set of a *Jenny Jones* TV show devoted
to women with big breasts. Pollock claimed the stripper
became angry when Pollock accused her of having received artificial implants. "She sexually assaulted me
with her breasts," said Pollock. "She banged me with
them in my eyes."

☞ In May 1993, to boost morale in war-torn Sarajevo, local
fashion designers and the Bosnian army organized a
"Miss Besieged Sarajevo" beauty pageant, even though a
few of the participants' bodies were marred by shrapnel
scars. During a procession onstage, the contestants held
a banner reading, in English, Don't Let Them Kill Us.
The seventeen-year-old winner, questioned by an Associated Press writer, responded, "Plans? I have no plans. I
may not even be alive tomorrow."

☞ A California appeals court in 1992 upheld a $100,000
award to the family of Wesley Wilkins from Wilkins's
former lover, Lillie Siplin. The appeals court agreed
with the trial court that Siplin had a legal duty to have
warned Wilkins before having sex with him that her
husband is a violent man. Siplin's husband, who had

become enraged toward his wife's previous lovers, broke in and stabbed Wilkins to death.

☞ Georgina Thompson, thirty-seven, was charged in Wellington, Kansas, in 1992 with soliciting two men to murder her common-law husband. The bounty she promised the men was her husband's collection of baseball cards—and she had given ten cards as a down payment. Said the deputy sheriff about the offer, "That's about as mean as a wife can get. The only thing lower would have been if she offered his hunting and fishing gear."

☞ Malaysian deputy interior minister Megat Junid Ayob told an antidrug conference in 1992 in Kuala Lumpur that shortages in heroin and cannabis had caused some addicts to get their necessary highs by sniffing fresh cow dung. Addicts put a coconut shell over the patty, with a hole at the top for sniffing.

☞ Actor Charles Peyton, who appears in X-rated films as Jeff Stryker, filed a lawsuit in Los Angeles in 1993 charging infringement of the "intellectual property" rights he owns in his name and person. Peyton accused the company that makes "Doc Johnson" marital aids of selling life-size rubber replicas of his penis without permission.

Not My Fault

☞ Claude Jones, thirty-two, confessed to conducting at least two dozen bank robberies around Sacramento, California, netting about $25,000, in order to finance his "addiction" to attending Los Angeles Raiders football games during the 1990-1991 season. In a letter to the judge, Jones wrote, "The Raiders were winning, and I began to believe that I was helping them by attending the games."

☞ In 1992, former securities broker Chris Christensen filed a complaint with a securities industry board, seeking $3 million in damages from his former employers, Shearson Lehman Brothers, Dean Witter Reynolds, and Prudential Securities. Christensen, who as a broker was the office star, says he lost over $1 million trading on his own account and that his employers not only failed to stop him from doing that but paid him so much money in bonuses that he felt encouraged to make even more bad trades.

☞ In 1993, former Northwestern University professor Olan Rand filed an employment discrimination complaint, claiming he was wrongfully fired after he pleaded guilty to theft of $33,000. He had continued to collect his mother's Social Security checks in their joint account for five years after her death in 1981. In his petition, he claims the university should not have dismissed him, since he suffered from the disability of "extreme procrastination behavior."

☞ Donald C. Winston, fired as a tenured instructor of English at Central Maine Technical College for sexually harassing an eighteen-year-old female student, fought for reinstatement by claiming he was handicapped, which is a protected status under state and federal law. He said he suffered from "a handicap of sexual addiction." (The Maine Supreme Court turned him down in 1993.)

☞ *The Wall Street Journal* reported in 1994 on a potential legal defense being considered by some well-to-do professionals who fail to file income tax returns. Such non-filers should be excused because they suffer from an anxiety syndrome characterized by "an overall inability to act in [their] own interest," according to a recent *New York Law Journal* article. Victims are "highly ambitious, hypercritical, detail-oriented people," according to a psychiatry professor, and thus cannot relax, don't know how to delegate, and tend to procrastinate and become secretive.

☞ According to records obtained by New York *Newsday,* New York City paid $30 million in 1992, and has paid $320 million since 1978, in damages to people who have merely fallen down on sidewalks. City law requires property owners to maintain sidewalks in front of their property, but the city gets sued for failure to enforce the law against procrastinating property owners.

Animals

☞ In Japan in 1992 Hamamatsu City Zoo officials began showing nonstop videos of gorilla-mating to "Daiko" to stimulate her interest in her mate, "Sho." After two weeks, officials reported that the two had started to have sex but that Daiko was not pregnant. (A zoo in Kyoto once claimed success in using a video to get a mother gorilla to breast-feed her young.) And *USA Today* reported in 1993 that Florida Wildlife Park officials planned to set up mirrors around six Caribbean flamingos because they believe they are more sexually excitable if in a group.

☞ *The Washington Post* reported in 1992 that the government of India had specially bred sixty-pound snapping turtles to reduce pollution in the holy Ganges River. Devout Hindus believe that the river will cause rebirth and eternal salvation to one's ashes, but some Hindu families cannot afford enough firewood for a total cremation. Thus, they throw in only partially cremated corpses, which clog the river (unless eaten by the turtles).

☞ Professor Lance Workman of Glamorgan University near Cardiff, Wales, reported in 1993 that his research, using a sonograph, shows that robins found around Sussex chirp in a different dialect (including pitch, lilt, and intonation) than robins of the same species found around Wales and that each assumes a defensive posture when exposed to the other's chirping.

☞ In 1993, the Pasadena, California, Humane Society constructed a $4.3 million dog-and-cat shelter, with towelled-lined cages, skylights, "microclimate" air conditioning, an aviary, sculptured bushes, "adoption counseling pavilions" in which people can meet with their prospective "companion animals," and, according to the architect, "a very subdued classical painting scheme."

☞ In 1992, in Maidenhead, England, the Society for the Prevention of Cruelty to Animals brought charges of pet abandonment against David Sharod, who had left his two exotic fish alone in their tank for three days while he was away. It cost the government about $12,000 to conduct a trial, and Sharod $3,000 to defend himself, before he was acquitted when he cited the society's own literature to show that fish could live comfortably on algae in the tank for up to two weeks.

☞ In 1993, Canadian environmentalist William Lishman and an associate flew two ultralight aircraft from Blackstock, Ontario, to Gaines, New York, and then to Airlie, Virginia, leading a flock of eighteen geese that had been raised in captivity and thus lacked skills on how to fly south for the winter.

☞ In 1994, *The Times* of London reported on a feud in the southern French town of Pia. Animal-rights activist Joelle Cinca happened to live next door to one of France's top pornographic film producers, Gerard Menoud, who sometimes would shoot sex scenes in his yard. Menoud claimed that the noise made by the geese Cinca kept in her garden disturbed his films' sound tracks; Cinca claimed that Menoud's actresses' loud orgasms had traumatized her geese.

☞ In late 1993, University of Massachusetts professor Robert Malloy announced a plan to save the endangered African black rhinoceros from hunters who kill them for their horns. At a cost of about $2,000 per animal, officials would tranquilize the rhino, remove the horn, and attach an artificial, colored one, using a technique similar to that used to affix dental crowns. Malloy argued that his plan is better than mere preventive removal because a horn, even an artificial one, is necessary for a rhino's social standing.

☞ In 1994, a thirty-three-pound, two-foot-long Border collie named Apple swallowed an entire twelve-inch carving knife in the course of snacking on devil's food cake at the home of her owner, Eric Fuchs of New York City. Two days after doctors removed the knife surgically, Apple was back at home, "ready to play," according to Fuchs.

Ingenious Products

☞ In the early 1990s, the London manufacturer Bodywise began selling the fragrance Aeolus 7 to bill collection agencies for about $6,000 a gram. Its main ingredient, the pheromone adrostenone, is secreted from men's armpits and groins and appears to be effective in tests in getting debtors to pay up. In a study in Australia, invoices mailed out that had been treated with Aeolus 7 had a 17 percent higher return than untreated bills.

☞ In 1992, San Francisco industrial chemist Merlyn Starley obtained a patent for "suspenders" to hold a condom in place so that it won't slip off during use. It is made of two plastic clips and a special adhesive attached to the wearer's legs.

☞ Danville, Virginia, inventor David Bivens, who developed large, irrigated brushes for washing cars and trucks (such as those found in commercial car washes), told the *Chicago Tribune* in 1992 that he had developed such a device for people. A person stands next to the brush and rubs against it as it makes 90 to 120 revolutions per minute, flicking off dirt and dead skin.

☞ A New Jersey environmental group, Clean Ocean Action, told the Associated Press in 1993 that it had manufactured and sold more than three hundred fishing lures that it made from tampon applicators that its members had found while cleaning the beaches. The "tampoons" sell for $6 each.

☞ Philip Middleton of Chantilly, Virginia, and his partner Richard Wooton marketed a commode for dogs in 1993. The dog walks up stairs at the side of the bathroom toilet, steps onto a platform over the toilet bowl, and squats down to use the Walk-Me-Not. And about the same time, an inventor in Southern California began marketing the Puppy Didy diaper for dogs.

☞ The German news agency Deutsche Presse Agentur reported in 1992 on Japanese inventor Kenji Kawakami's "New Idea Academy," which featured among his most successful products a portable washing machine that straps onto the user's leg; a traveling necktie with room for writing utensils and a calculator; padded booties for cats so they can dust the floor while walking around; a "solar flashlight" that provides a strong beam of light as long as the sun is shining; and a rack worn on your back, secured by a shoulder brace, on which "clothing can be hung to dry while you bicycle about."

☞ The Associated Press reported in 1992 that landscaper Jay Knudsen of Des Moines, Iowa, ran a side business in which relatives of deceased hunters paid him to load the deceased's ashes into shotgun shells and fire at targets as the deceased might have wanted it. Knudsen said he also gets requests to put ashes in duck decoys, fishermen's lures, and golf clubs. Said Knudsen, "There's a lot of ideas that go to waste because people are afraid to be laughed at."

☞ Among the products brought to market in the early 1990s: handcrafted dog beds (starting at $900, plus another $250 for the draperies to hang from the four-poster models) from the New York designer Joseph Biunno; "Fudge on Fire," fudge laced with hot peppers, from the Fudge Farm in Paso Robles, California; caskets customized in colors of Southeastern Conference football teams, from Loretto Casket Company in Tennessee; and a hair dressing that gives clean hair the look and feel of hair that "hasn't been washed in three days," from the Los Angeles company Rusk.

The Best of the Rest

WELL STATED

☞ In 1992 some of the 280 survivors of a Dutch charter plane that had recently crashed in a wind gust in the resort town of Faro, Portugal, gathered to tell their stories to reporters. Wim Kodman, twenty-seven, who is a botanist, said he was trying to calm a friend during the wind turbulence by appealing to logic. Said Kodman, "I told him, 'I'm a scientist—we're objective.' I told him a crash was improbable. I was trying to remember the exact probability when we smashed into the ground."

☞ Mary Hodgdon, a false-teeth user, was fired by the Mount Mansfield resort in Vermont in 1987 and sued the company for handicap discrimination. Mount Mansfield defended the firing by showing that it was attempting to move up to a four-star status and that Hodgdon often worked, visible to customers, without her teeth because she said they were painful. Wrote the resort management, "Employees [are] expected to have teeth and wear them daily to work."

☞ Steven L. Johnson, forty, sentenced to two years in prison in Brookings, South Dakota, in 1992 for drunk driving, explained to the judge, "I enjoyed drinking while driving. It's one of the most pleasurable habits I've had."

EUNUCHS CONVENE IN INDIA
[with apologies to the great Ivan M. Katz, Esq., for the heading]

☞ In 1994, an AIDS activist organization in Madras, India, made a public plea that eunuchs, who were convening for their annual festival near the city, use condoms during their wild celebration. Many of the country's 400,000 eunuchs retain their penises, and Community Action Network estimated that ten thousand sex acts would take place by the close of the fifteen-day gathering. An AIDS activist said that because most of the eunuchs were recruited by force, they lead "angry" lives and thus show little restraint in their sexual activity.

CLICHÉS COME TO LIFE

☞ James "Bubba" Wilson, twenty, filed a lawsuit in 1994 in Rockwood, Tennessee, for $10.7 million against the Rockwood police for false arrest. Wilson claims police were looking for a drug suspect named "Bubba," approached him on the porch of his mother's home, asked if he was "Bubba," and took him into custody when he said yes. Wilson was released shortly afterward when police realized he was the wrong "Bubba." According to the lawsuit, "Bubba" is the most common name in Rockwood.

☞ Shortly after 2 P.M. on May 23, 1994, in Pomona, California, Tamika Johnson, nineteen, was issued a jaywalking ticket for making a dangerous street crossing in front of a county building. Minutes later, after the officer left, Johnson tried the crossing again, was hit by a car, and suffered a broken leg.

FIRST THINGS FIRST

☞ In 1991, Donald DeGreve, sixty-five, suffered a fatal
heart attack while playing golf in Winter Haven, Florida.
As his body lay on the sixteenth green covered with a
sheet, and while course officials tried to contact his
wife and funeral home personnel, a steady stream of
DeGreve's friends, playing in the Swiss Village Mobile
Home Park league, passed from the fifteenth green to
the seventeenth tee to continue their games. "Life goes
on," said one man.

TACKY, TACKY

☞ In 1993, opera singer Luciano Pavarotti was accused by
the author of an art book of copying her drawings and
offering them for sale under his name. One painting,
which Pavarotti told an interviewer was so touching to
him that he cried when he painted it, was allegedly so
faithfully copied that it included the original artist's
errors in scenic detail.

☞ In 1994, the Phoenix, Arizona, *New Times* published an unidentified man's detailed list of pros and cons about his two girlfriends, Brenda and Dominique, that had been accidentally discarded in a magazine pocket on an Air Reno flight and that the newspaper had obtained. Despite Brenda's "Wealthy" and "Nice car" versus Dominique's "Chipping teeth" and "Cuts me down," Dominique appeared to have the upper hand on the list, which was scrawled on bookkeeping ledger sheets. Dominique had eighteen pros and eleven cons, versus Brenda's fifteen and twenty-two, respectively, and "I love her" appeared No. 3 under Dominique but only No. 15 under Brenda. Besides, Brenda's No. 9 con is "She's married." ("Brenda" and "Dominique" were pseudonyms supplied by *New Times*.)

☞ In 1994, Los Angeles talk-show host Joe Crummey put on sale a thirty-minute video of his recent brain surgery. The $22.50 tape, made by St. Vincent Medical Center staff, includes interviews with Crummey's doctors and Crummey's station colleagues.

FUTURE WEIRDO

☞ In October 1993, Mikey Sproul, age three, made national news when he commandeered the family car, which had one flat tire, and cruised down U.S. 41 near Tampa, Florida, hitting two parked cars and narrowly missing several moving ones. Mikey's assessment at that time was, "I go zoom." One month later and less widely reported nationally, Mikey, using a cigarette lighter, burned down his family's house, sending his father to the hospital with second- and third-degree burns. Mikey's assessment then: "Now I have no more house."

I DON'T THINK SO

☞ Brazilian legislator João Alves, who was the subject of a 1993 corruption investigation because he had amassed the equivalent of $51 million on only a legislator's salary, told a congressional panel that he accumulated his wealth by winning national bingo and local and national lotteries a total of twenty-four thousand times between 1988 and 1993.

☞ Philadelphia orthodontist Warren Graboyes filed an insurance claim in 1992, demanding $5,000 a month for his "disability" of "frotteurism," which is the compulsion to touch another's private parts. (Graboyes, a.k.a. "Dr. Touchy," was not working at the time because he had been convicted the year before of fondling teenage female patients, and evidence suggested he had been doing it for nineteen years.)

☞ Elmwood Park, New Jersey, principal Samuel R. Bracigliano, forty-nine, on trial in 1991 for molesting teenage boys, repeatedly denied that the extensive pornography collection seized from his home was for his sexual pleasure. However, found with the pornography was a jar of Vaseline along with pieces of paper in videotape boxes that contained numbers that corresponded to the VCR counter numbers at which sex scenes begin. Bracigliano said he was a serious photographer of nudes: "I was doing my best work yet when I was arrested."

☞ From the Police Reports column of the *Glen Ellyn* [Illinois] *Press* of December 19, 1991: Eric Hoyt, twenty-one, and Peter A. Thordason, twenty-five, were charged with stealing Christmas trees from a food store lot. However, the two denied they intended to steal the trees: "Thordason allegedly told police he wanted to see how long it would take him to run around the building carrying each tree while Hoyt timed him."

IN THE WRONG PLACE AT THE WRONG TIME

☞ Mireya Funair, thirty, was hospitalized in 1994 after being trapped for forty minutes in her car buried up to her neck in concrete. A cement truck had tipped over, and the truck's funnel had punctured the top of Funair's car, slowly pouring concrete directly into it.

WELL, SURE!

☞ Alphonso Johnson Quinn, thirty-six, was convicted of being the Bowie, Maryland, "crossbow rapist" who had terrorized several women in their homes around 1993. According to police chief David Mitchell, Quinn's crimes benefited his day job: He sold "home security systems," and his sales literature referred to the need for protection from the crossbow rapist.

☞ According to the December 1993 *State Legislatures* magazine, Kansas was toughening its worker compensation laws because a physician on the worker compensation agency staff had filed a claim, alleging that he suffered back pains from having to sit so much on cramped witness stands while testifying in worker compensation cases.

☞ *The New York Times* reported in 1992 that the Environmental Protection Agency, asked to respond officially to a congressional report charging that the agency uses too many outside contractors, paid a contractor $20,000 to write the response.

NOT HAPPY UNLESS THEY'RE NOT HAPPY

☞ For months before the 1994 Winter Olympics, Olympics employees in Lillehammer, Norway, trained with "smile holders" to improve their cheerfulness during the Games. A smile holder is a device that fits on the wearer's head, with clips that grasp the corners of the wearer's mouth; it can be adjusted, by pulling a strap, to go from slight grin to gleeful smile.

LAST DAYS OF THE PLANET

☞ A recent, semi-official student pamphlet of George Mason University in Fairfax, Virginia, explained that freedom from discrimination includes gays' and lesbians' "right" not to be stood too far away from during conversations with straights, and minority students' "right" not to have white students act surprised when a minority student performs a task well.

☞ On December 17, 1991, the Communist Party in Beijing issued a proclamation against excessive holiday cheer during the new year's season. Included were admonitions against "spending" and other wastefulness (subject to fines) and against any consumption of more than "a cup of tea" at year-end parties.

☞ *The Washington Post* reported in 1993 on the nine-year-old war between India and Pakistan over claim to the Siachen Glacier in the Himalaya Mountains. The countries have largely resolved other parts of their forty-six-year-old border dispute, but the battle over the glacier continues, despite its uninhabitability and the casualty rate: For every soldier who falls to hostile gunfire, nine soldiers die from the blinding blizzards, the treacherous footing on the ice-encrusted peaks, and windchills reaching more than 150 degrees below zero.

OUR CONSTITUTIONAL RIGHTS

☞ In 1994, Jams Von Arx, forty-one, who had been on probation for child molestation in Wausau, Wisconsin, was jailed after he refused court-ordered sex therapy designed to induce interest in adult erotic images. He argued that such therapy is unconstitutional because it requires him to masturbate, which is against his religion.

FAMILY VALUES

☞ In 1994, elementary school teacher Myra Obasi, twenty-nine, of Shreveport, Louisiana, was brought, bleeding from the eyes, to Parkland Memorial Hospital in Dallas by her two sisters, who eventually were charged with having gouged out Obasi's eyes with their fingers because they thought she was possessed by the spirit of her father. Detectives were unable to question Obasi for several hours because she refused to stop chanting, "Thank you, Jesus."

115

The Concrete Enema

☞ In 1993, in Oxnard, California, Dale Chester, twenty-two, was sentenced to three years in prison for raping the pregnant girlfriend of his brother Ruben. Dale's brothers Leonard, thirty-two, and Samuel, twenty-nine, were serving long prison terms for the violent rapes of five women in separate incidents, and Ruben, twenty-four, was serving time for robbery and assault. Their father is a local pastor and their mother a Christian missionary, and police and prosecutors said there was no evidence of the childhood abuse that typically portends such adult violence.

OUR ELECTED OFFICIALS

☞ Among mayoral results in November 1993: Friendsville, Maryland, mayor Spencer Schlosnagle was reelected (in February 1994) though he had been convicted a week before of indecent exposure and had four other such charges pending. And Hialeah, Florida, voters elected Raul Martinez mayor, though he was awaiting sentencing on federal extortion charges. (In 1971, Hialeah also voted in as mayor a recently convicted felon.)

☞ In 1994, a surveillance camera revealed Florida state representative Carlos Valdes as the man defacing the walls of a condominium complex in Miami with a black marker, and who is suspected of being the one responsible for several other episodes of graffiti vandalism. Said Valdes, "I can only characterize my actions as embarrassing and unacceptable."

CHUTZPAH

☞ For most of 1991, California's employment disability agency paid wealthy physician Gershon Hepner of Century City $266 a month on his stress claim, even though the prosecutor said Hepner's "stress" was merely that brought on by his having gotten caught on fraud, grand theft, and tax evasion charges (to which he pleaded guilty and for which he is awaiting sentencing). State law entitled Hepner to the money because another physician certified that the stress was "job-related."

QUESTIONABLE JUDGMENT

☞ Ronald Sturkes was charged in Hicksville, New York, in 1992 with irregularities in taking his driver's license test. After becoming well known to motor vehicle department employees by vigorously protesting his failure on the driving portion of the test, Sturkes—twenty-seven years old and white—allegedly arranged for a fifty-five-year-old black man to impersonate him in taking the written test.

CULTURAL DIVERSITY

☞ In 1992, critics in India's western state of Maharashtra called an end to a traditional annual event in which women from the adjacent villages of Sukhed and Bor line up on opposite sides of a canal and on a given signal yell insults at each other. (The event commemorates a feud between two wives who lived in separate villages but were married to the same chief.)

☞ In 1992, town councilors in Hearst, Ontario, ended the long-time ritual of requiring prospective bridegrooms to be locked in cages for a day in the center of town, on public display. The tradition usually goes no further than allowing the townspeople to throw eggs and tomatoes at the men for a price—in part to help the couple get started financially—but a few years ago, in an extreme case, one man was given an enema with a grease gun. Local clergy advised the councilors that some men so fear the prospect that they decline marriage altogether.

☞ In Cairo, Egypt, in 1994, seven Muslim fundamentalist lawyers filed a lawsuit to force happily married Professor Nasr Abu Zeid and his wife to divorce because Zeid had written alleged heresies that disqualified him from marriage to a Muslim woman. According to the lawyers, any Muslim has the power to petition to end such a marriage. The controversy proved to be a watershed case in which the outsider-complaint route to divorce began losing validity among Muslims.

OOPS!

☞ Among highway truck spills over the last few years: near Levittown, New York, in 1992, mayonnaise; near Manila in 1992, coconut oil; near Shelby, North Carolina, in 1993, chocolate syrup; near Hampton, Illinois, in 1993, hamburger; and near Pataskala, Ohio, in 1993, glue. In Kansas City, Missouri, in 1992, a truck carrying remaindered pornographic magazines to a recycling center overturned on a busy street, causing opportunistic drivers to create a rush-hour traffic jam as they scrambled for the cargo.

☞ In 1993, a young couple had to be treated for hypothermia in Gernsheim, Germany, after the parked car in which they were having sex rolled down a boat ramp into the Rhine River.

☞ *Ring* magazine reported that boxer Daniel Caruso, moments before the bell to begin his New York City Golden Gloves fight in 1992, tried to psyche himself up by using the method employed by former champion Marvin Hagler: pounding his gloves into his face. Caruso broke his nose, forcing cancellation of the fight.

☞ In 1991, workers in Blackpool, England, draining the lake that lies under a resort's roller-coaster ride, discovered "hundreds" of pairs of false teeth, several wigs, and six glass eyes.

☞ About fifteen customers had gathered their grocery items at a Safeway in Oxon Hill, Maryland, shortly after 10 A.M. on Christmas morning in 1993 and were lined up at the checkout lanes, but no cashiers were on duty, and no one answered calls at the back of the store. Local police were called and after investigating found that the store was supposed to be closed but that the Christmas Eve crew had accidentally left the lights on and the doors unlocked, giving shoppers the impression it was open for business.

☞ In 1993, a man whose name was withheld by reporters was rescued by firefighters after spending the night in the pit of an outhouse at a boat landing near Eugene, Oregon. The man claimed that he had been high after sniffing glue, had heard someone calling for help from the pit, and had fallen in while looking for him.

☞ In 1993, for the second time in less than three years, the Air Force revealed that it had lost an $18 million F-16 fighter plane because the pilot was unable to control the aircraft while using his "piddle pack" during in-flight urination. (Both pilots ejected safely.)

MEDICAL

☞ Officials of the Shriners Burn Institute at the University of Cincinnati disclosed in 1992 that one of its surgeons, Dr. Glenn D. Warden, once carved his initials and a tic-tac-toe diagram into the skull of a dying infant and drew "happy faces" onto surgery patients' genitalia with a marking pen. Warden, who was scheduled to become president of a national surgeons' association, said that he had only been trying to lighten the atmosphere of the operating room.

☞ *New York Newsday* reported in 1993 that a forty-six-year-old Worcester, Massachusetts, man inexplicably began speaking with a French accent immediately after he was involved in an automobile accident. Dr. Majis Moonis told the annual meeting of the American Academy of Neurology that about two dozen cases of "foreign accent syndrome" have been reported in this century, caused by a change in the brain circuit involved with motor control that affects the vocal cords.

☞ In Grants Pass, Oregon, in 1993, Michael Kennedy tried to shoot a beer can off Anthony Roberts's head with a bow and arrow in what Roberts later described as an initiation rite for "Mountain Men Anonymous." The arrow went through Roberts's right eye, penetrated eight inches of brain, and came within a millimeter of severing major blood vessels that would have caused instant death. Roberts never lost consciousness, was later fitted with a glass eye, and suffered no diminution of brain function (from however much brain function he had previously that led him to consent to being an archer's target).

☞ And one week after that, an errant eight-foot-long javelin thrown during warm-ups at a high school track meet in New Brunswick, New Jersey, went completely through the neck of Jeremy Campbell, fifteen, manager of his school's track team, but missed vital organs by millimeters, enabling Campbell to be up and about the next day. About twelve inches of the spear protruded through the other side of Campbell's neck.

☞ And one day after that, dairy farmer Anthony Tworek, thirty-one, slipped from a stepladder in Clarksdale, Missouri, falling backward with such force that he impaled himself by the neck on a 1¹/₂-inch-thick pole. The pole entered alongside his carotid artery but did not touch it and went through the roof of his mouth, missing his brain by half an inch. He, too, fully recovered.

☞ California attorney general Dan Lungren proposed in 1993 that the state prove that cyanide gas has pain-numbing qualities—in order to demonstrate that the gas chamber is not "cruel and unusual" punishment as charged by its critics. To show the pain-numbing qualities, Lungren proposed that the state put rats in pain by "colon balloon distension"—inserting balloons in the anuses of 60 rats and inflating them until the rats squeal—and then administering cyanide at different doses to see if the pain subsides.

☞ In 1994, pediatric orthopedist William Zink of Orlando, Florida, was detained by authorities on charges of fondling young boys who were his patients. One mother had complained that in the course of thirty-five office visits by her son for foot problems, the boy was given gloveless rectal exams fifteen times; another said her son received a rectal exam before surgery on an ingrown toenail. Zink's attorney said the charges reflect differences in "interpretation of the way he practices medicine. You are going to have a difference of opinion."

NAMES IN THE NEWS

☞ Police in State College, Pennsylvania, charged a nineteen-year-old woman with provoking a riot early one Sunday morning in 1992. A crowd of more than one thousand people had become unruly after gathering to watch at a window as the woman and her male companion undressed in their bedroom. The house was on Beaver Street, and arrested was Elizabeth Ann Apinis.

☞ The vice president of the chamber of commerce in Clinton, Missouri, announced in 1992 she was voting Republican. The veep, Georgianna Bush, goes by "George."

☞ A 1993 Associated Press dispatch from Australia reported that members of Parliament traditionally address each other much more aggressively than members of Congress do in the United States. Among the names recently overheard on the floor of the Parliament: perfumed gigolos, brain-damaged, harlot, sleazebag, scumbag, mental patient, and dog's vomit.

☞ The trade association International Business Forms Industries, Inc., changed its name in 1993 to The International Association Serving the Forms, Information Management, Systems Automation, and Printed Communications Requirements of Business.

☞ The real name of the fifty-year-old man, charged in West Haven, Connecticut, in 1992 with having offered to pay a Yale University female student's tuition (totaling $26,000) if she would spank him, was revealed to be Alexander Bizzario. (He had lured her to his home to fill out grant applications but told police later that he had no grant authority.)

☞ Ronald Hodges, thirty-four, was arrested in New Orleans in 1992 and charged with murder but was released a short time later when police learned that the suspect they wanted was his brother, whose given name is Ronnie Hodges. Said Ronald, "That's the way our mother named us."

☞ Tiverton, Nova Scotia, resident Annabel Elliott Outhouse, author of a book on outdoor toilets called *Outhouses of the Island* [Long Island in Nova Scotia], hosted an Outhouse family reunion in 1992 attended by 300 people from Canada and the United States. (Outhouse is the most common surname on Long Island.)

BOTTOM OF THE GENE POOL

☞ Gary Blantz, twenty-nine, was arrested for kidnapping a bar owner near Lancaster, Pennsylvania, in 1992. Police reported later that Blantz shot himself in the foot with his .45-caliber revolver in order to show the victim what would happen to him if he disobeyed.

☞ A thirty-eight-year-old man, unidentified in news reports, was hospitalized in Princeton, West Virginia, in 1992 after he shot himself accidentally three times—as he attempted to clean each of his three guns. He said the first shot didn't hurt, the second "stung a little," and the third "really hurt," prompting him to call an ambulance.

☞ George Gibbs, twenty-three, suffered second- and third-degree burns on his head in Columbus, Ohio, in 1994. He had diagnosed his car's problem as a frozen fuel line, which he thought he could correct by running warm gasoline through it. He then tried to heat a two-gallon can of gasoline on a gas stove.

☞ In a Fort Lauderdale, Florida, court in 1994, accused murderer Donald Leroy Evans, thirty-eight, filed a motion asking permission to wear a Ku Klux Klan robe in the courtroom and to be referred to in legal documents by "the honorable and respected name of Hi Hitler." According to courthouse employees interviewed by the Associated Press, Evans thought Adolf Hitler's followers were saying "Hi Hitler" rather than "Heil, Hitler."

THE CONCRETE ENEMA

ENEMA

And Other News
of the Weird Classics

The Concrete Enema

Oh, man! Almost forgot. Need one more story. Like, the story. Like, why was the book titled *The Concrete Enema* if none of the previous three hundred or so stories was about a concrete enema?

(Well, actually, the book was titled *The Concrete Enema* largely because the editor at the publishing house thought it would be a neat line on his résumé, and the publisher's marketing people needed a pizzazzy title to work with, and booksellers could use a little help in remembering the book, and deejays in most cities certainly won't mind plugging a title like that on the air, and so forth.)

The question I am most frequently asked is whether weird news is weird anymore to me, or do I just mechanically, half asleep, lay out the stories every week. Actually, a week never passes without my noticing at least one person or event that represents a genuine advance in bizarreness. "Advance," though, is usually just a short-term, ten-octane thrust. However, there was one week in 1989 when I was jet-propelled around the track. That was when Weird News-ranger Tim Reade sent me a short case report by two physicians from a 1987 issue of *The American Journal of Forensic Medicine and Pathology.*

The physicians began innocuously enough: "During the last twenty years, sexual habits have changed in Western society." Hoooo, boy!

A guy checked into an emergency room and preferred not to sit. The doctor's digital examination of the rectum indicated a "stony hard mass." The guy had heard that the process of concrete's hardening gave a pleasurable sensation in the rectum, and he and a companion had arranged to administer to him an enema made of concrete mix. (Even assuming a grand rectal sensation, this would be the single worst example I have ever heard of the perils of short-term thinking; I mean, forget all about getting this guy to open a savings account or refrain from scratching a scab.)

Through the miracles of modern medicine, a concrete chunk (about 5" x 2" x 2", weighing about ten ounces) was removed intact, yielding "a perfect concrete cast of the rectum," as if it were ready to go straight to Johns Hopkins as a visual aid in Proctology 101. The only defect in the cast was chipping at one end, revealing a Ping-Pong ball (which the doctors theorize was used as a stopper to retain the enema, but which suggests a failure of the patient to grasp the concept that he's dealing with concrete and thus might not really need a stopper).

The physicians report that they recommended psychological counseling, but that the patient declined and left the hospital on his own the next day.

I know a few people who have as a hobby ritually attempting to appear in person at the major events of the times—inaugurations, Super Bowls, award ceremonies, etc.—but I've never considered doing that. However, I would give plenty to have been in the room with our two enema friends (1) at the time they decided that, yeah, that's a neat idea, we'll mix up a batch of concrete and run it down a funnel—just like cement-mixer trucks have—into my rectum!; (2) at the time it first begins to dawn on the cementee that perhaps he's made a mistake, and that, truly, things are only going to get worse in the next few minutes as the concrete irreversibly hardens; and (3) as he heads off for the hospital trying to compose his explanation for the doctor (e.g., fell buttfirst off a roof, naked, into a vat

The	of wet cement? inadvisably laughed at some burly workers
Concrete	while passing a construction site? had to try something new
Enema	since Imodium AD didn't do a bit of good?).

Chuck Shepherd
June 1996

About the Author

Chuck Shepherd is the author of *News of the Weird*, a weekly collection of the best bizarre-but-true news stories, which is syndicated in more than 200 newspapers.

He has also been a magazine editor, a federal government lawyer, a criminal-defense lawyer, and a professor at the George Washington University business school.